# A Closer Look

## 52 Not-So-Ordinary Devotions for Those Who Love the Word of God

KRESS
BIBLICAL
RESOURCES

*A Closer Look: 52 Not-So-Ordinary Devotions for Those Who Love the Word of God*

Published by:

 KRESS BIBLICAL RESOURCES

www.kressbiblical.com

ISBN: 978-1-934952-47-4

# Contents

5

# Preface—Don't Skip

A wise pastor and faithful expositor who reviewed parts of this book advised that a preface be written to caution and prepare the reader for what follows. He wrote:

1) There are some novel interpretations, as you noted.

2) Those I've read made good exegetical cases for the possibility of the proposed interpretation, and some good insights are offered.

3) Expositors should aim at CERTAINTY—though we may not always attain to it, it should always be our aim. Even though we could make a case that "this probably alludes to this," if we aren't certain of it, it remains in the realm of speculation.

4) I always try to remember that I'm not just teaching people, I'm teaching people how to arrive at truth through their study of Scripture, and how to teach others. In other words, what I might do in moderation, and with a whole lot of experience behind me, someone else might do to excess and with ZERO experience under his or her belt. To say it another way, you know how to do what you've done here and not take it too far—are you confident if your readers do the same, they will land in safe places?

5) So, what if you wrote a clear preface that identifies pitfalls, gives caution to readers, etc.?

His words are a good warning.

First Timothy 1:4 sounds an even graver warning against those who devote themselves to myths and endless genealogies, which result in controversies and speculations.

Therefore, it must be noted that this book is meant to promote careful observation and exegetical scrutiny of passages and details that are either overlooked, or too often taken for granted. In turn, this should lead to praise to the God who inspired the Scriptures and gave them as a gift to His people. This praise should culminate in love for Him and a desire to point others to Him.

Faithful Bible students may disagree with some of the exegetical decisions and nuanced interpretations in this book, but these chapters are put forth with a desire to encourage God's people to look closely at God's Word and rejoice in God's grace as they do.

It is certain that God loves His people and has graced them with His Word—in every detail. It is also certain that the point of Scripture is to reveal God's plan of salvation, which is through faith in His Son Jesus Christ (2 Tim. 3:15)—resulting in the praise of the glory of God's grace (Eph. 1:6, 12, 14), and love for God and man (Matt. 22:37-40; 1 Tim. 1:5). To that end, this book is offered to the reader.

With these cautions and caveats in mind, take a closer look at *A Closer Look.*

# 1

## Jesus and Jacob's Ladder

### *Gen. 28:12-13a; 17b*

12  [Jacob] had a dream, and behold, a ladder was set on the earth with its top reaching to heaven; and behold, **the angels of God were ascending and descending on it**.

13  And behold, the LORD stood above it …

17  … This is none other than the house of God, and this is the gate of heaven."

### *Gen. 32:27-28*

27  So he said to him, "What is your name?" And he said, "Jacob."

28  He said, "Your name shall no longer be Jacob, but Israel; for you have striven with God and with men and have prevailed."

### John 1:47-51

47  Jesus saw Nathanael coming to Him, and said of him, "Behold, an **Israelite** indeed, in whom there is no **deceit!**"

48  Nathanael said to Him, "How do You know me?" Jesus answered and said to him, "Before Philip called you, when you were under the fig tree, I saw you."

49  Nathanael answered Him, "Rabbi, You are the Son of God; You are the King of Israel."

50  Jesus answered and said to him, "Because I said to you that I saw you under the fig tree, do you believe? You will see greater things than these."

51  And He said to him, "Truly, truly, I say to you, you will see the heavens opened and **the angels of God ascending and descending on the Son of Man**."

When Nathanael met Jesus for the first time, he came as a bit of a skeptic. But Jesus changed his mind with two simple statements. Nathanael's self-righteous doubt was transformed into a stunning declaration of Jesus as Messiah. Why?

Just prior to actually interacting with the Lord, Philip had told Nathanael that they had found the One "of whom Moses in the Law and also the Prophets wrote—Jesus of Nazareth ..." (John 1:45). Nathanael immediately replied, "Can any good thing come out of Nazareth?" (John 1:46). In other words, Nathanael clearly doubted that the Messiah would come from such a disreputable place—at least in his estimation.

Yet, when Jesus said: "Behold, an Israelite indeed, in whom there is no deceit," Nathanael was intrigued and asked, "How do You know me?" To which, Jesus replied, "Before Philip called you, when you were under the fig tree, I saw you." At that point Nathanael didn't simply say, "I'd like to hear more"—but rather, "Rabbi, You are the Son of God; You are the King of Israel." Again, why such a dramatic change?

Elsewhere, "under the fig tree" speaks of peace and safety (cf. 1 Kings 4:25; Micah 4:4; Zech. 3:10). Some commentators believe that the expression, "under the fig tree" was a Jewish idiom for meditating on the Scriptures. Though we can't be certain, the context of this passage indicates that Nathanael had been "under the fig tree" (either literally, or figuratively), evidently thinking about Genesis 27-28, which includes God's revelation of Himself, His promises, and the very gateway of heaven in spite of Jacob's *deceit* in stealing the patriarchal blessing and flight in fear for his life.

Jacob—the *deceiver*—was later renamed, "*Israel*"—one who wrestled with God. Renamed by a mysterious "man" who was actually God (Gen. 32:28; cf. 35:10—at Bethel). Jesus called Nathanael, "an *Israelite* indeed in whom there is no *deceit*"— clear allusions to Genesis 27-28, 32, and 35.

This man from Nazareth was addressing the very issues Nathanael had been wrestling with. So Nathanael asked cautiously, "How do you know me?" Jesus then confirmed His supernatural knowledge by saying essentially, "Before we even met, I knew what you were doing and thinking"—i.e., wrestling with God about Genesis 27-28—Jacob, his deceit and the stairway to heaven, etc.

Nathanael was immediately convinced that Jesus the Nazarene was indeed the promised One—the Davidic "Son of God" and the promised King of Israel.

Christ didn't stop at Nathanael's confession that He is Messiah. Jesus said: "Because I said to you that I saw you under the fig tree, do you believe? You will see greater things than these … Truly, truly I say to you, you will see the heavens opened and **the angels of God ascending and descending on the Son of Man**." This man from Nazareth is not only the promised Messiah-King, He is the divine bridge between heaven and earth—the dwelling place of God and the gateway to heaven (see Gen. 28:12, 17; cf. Daniel 7:13-14).[1]

The Lord knew Jacob's deceit and yet revealed His Person, His promises, and His amazing grace to him. Jesus knew Nathanael's self-righteousness (not being from Nazareth), his skepticism—his every thought. And He revealed Himself and His grace to such a man.

Jesus knows our every thought, our every deceit, our every self-righteous assessment, our questions, our skepticism—and yet in grace, He still calls us to believe and embrace Him as both King and God, and the only gateway to heaven. Do *you* believe?

---

[1] If, as many commentators believe, the grammar indicates that the angels were descending on Jacob—the point is much the same. If Jacob was a special object of divine selection and heavenly activity—the disciples would soon see that Jesus is the ultimate in such divine privilege and selection in God's redemptive plan.

# 2

## A Mystery Revealed—Yet Not Fully Understood

### Isaiah 48:12-16

12     "Listen to Me, O Jacob, even Israel whom I called;
       I am He, I am the first, I am also the last.
13     "Surely My hand founded the earth,
       And My right hand spread out the heavens;
       When I call to them, they stand together.
14     "Assemble, all of you, and listen!
       Who among them has declared these things?
       The LORD loves him; he will carry out His good pleasure on
          Babylon,
       And His arm *will be against* the Chaldeans.
15     "I, even I, have spoken; indeed I have called him,
       I have brought him, and He will make his ways successful.
16     "Come near to Me, listen to this:
       From the first I have not spoken in secret,
       From the time it took place, I was there.
       And now the Lord GOD has sent Me, and His Spirit."

Indications of the plurality within the Godhead are scattered throughout the Old Testament (e.g., Gen. 1:1-2, 26-27; Ex. 23:20-21), but rarely are there specific references to the *Trinity* of the One true God outside of the New Testament. Isaiah 48:12-16, however, is an Old Testament passage that does seem to point to a mysterious union between three distinct Persons (see also Is. 11:1-5; 42:1; 59:19-21; 61:1; 63:7-14).

Verses 12-14a clearly identify deity as speaking—calling Israel to listen. The second half of verse 14 seems to be a prophetic reference to Cyrus, the Persian king who would come and destroy Babylonian rule (cf. 45:1). Then verses 15-16ab again clearly indicate divine speech.

The words, "I have brought him, and he will make his ways successful" could refer to God's providence in raising up Cyrus, and *Cyrus'* own determined success in defeating Babylon. But this would be out of character with the tenor of the passage—God's sovereign power in bringing His plan to pass.

Another explanation might be to see "he will make his ways successful" as simply the insertion of a narrator's voice at this point. Perhaps—but could it be in light of the second half of verse 16, there is a distinct Person who will make Cyrus successful?

Notice v. 16c: "From the time it took place, I was there." The language is reminiscent of the personification of the wisdom of God found in Proverbs 8:22-31. The final phrase of verse 16 reads: "And now the LORD God has sent Me and His Spirit."

Some explain this as a rather abrupt insertion of the prophet Isaiah's voice. But it is difficult to find Isaiah speaking of himself in this literary unit (chap. 42-53). And it is difficult to see him saying, "From the time it took place, I was there." The speaker hints at, if not claims, pre-existence (perhaps even eternality in light verse 12).

As well, it would appear very out of place for a yet unborn Cyrus to speak, indicating pre-existence—and as being sent by the Holy Spirit. Granted, this could be attributed to the prophetic (and nearly poetic) genre—but it seems unlikely.

Wouldn't it be easier to explain the mysterious change in speakers as a shift from God, to His Servant (i.e., God the Son)? Note the similar language that clearly references the Son of God/Servant in Isaiah 61:1: "The Spirit of the Lord God is upon me, because the LORD has anointed me to bring good news to the afflicted; He has sent me ..." (cf. Luke 4:18-19).

As well, the immediate literary unit, chapters 42-53, is filled with prophecies of this glorious, yet mysterious Servant of

Yahweh who ultimately accomplishes Yahweh's purposes and redeems Yahweh's people (e.g., 42:1ff; 49:3-6; 52:12; 53:11).

Notably, this Servant is not only mysteriously pre-existent and connected to God and His Spirit, Isaiah 49 will reveal that He is identified as Israel, yet distinct from Israel (but that is for another study).

There is New Testament data, which supports the conclusion here that the pronouns and language in Isaiah 48:12-16 identify distinct Persons within the One True God. Revelation 1:17-18 clearly identifies Jesus with this Old Testament passage. It reads: "… Do not be afraid; **I am the first and the last**, and the living One; and I was dead, and behold, I am alive forevermore, and I have the keys of death and Hades" (cf. Rev. 1:8; 2:8; 22:11).

Questions remain to be sure, but as we have seen here, Isaiah 48:12-16 seems to identify Yahweh as sending His pre-existing Agent and His Spirit to accomplish His plan.

Praise God for the mystery of the Trinity—revealed yet not fully understood by creatures, so that the Creator may be worshiped and adored for eternity, as we continue to plumb the depths of His glory.

# 3

## Water into Wine

### John 2:1-11

1   On the third day there was a wedding in Cana of Galilee, and the mother of Jesus was there;

2   and both Jesus and His disciples were invited to the wedding.

3   When the wine ran out, the mother of Jesus said to Him, "They have no wine."

4   And Jesus said to her, "Woman, what does that have to do with us? My hour has not yet come."

5   His mother said to the servants, "Whatever He says to you, do it."

6   Now there were six stone waterpots set there for the Jewish custom of purification, containing twenty or thirty gallons each.

7   Jesus said to them, "Fill the waterpots with water." So they filled them up to the brim.

8   And He said to them, "Draw some out now and take it to the headwaiter." So they took it to him.

9   When the headwaiter tasted the water which had become wine, and did not know where it came from (but the servants who had drawn the water knew), the headwaiter called the bridegroom,

10  and said to him, "Every man serves the good wine first, and when the people have drunk freely, then he serves the poorer wine; but you have kept the good wine until now."

11  This beginning of His signs Jesus did in Cana of Galilee, and manifested His glory, and His disciples believed in Him.

### Gen. 49:10-11

10  "The scepter shall not depart from Judah,
Nor the ruler's staff from between his feet,
Until Shiloh comes,
And to him shall be the obedience of the peoples.

11  "He ties his foal to the vine,
And his donkey's colt to the choice vine;
He washes his garments in wine,
And his robes in the blood of grapes.

Often when we hear of Jesus turning water into wine, we think of His creative power as God the Son. And certainly there is truth in such an assessment. But is that all that John wanted to convey as he penned the second chapter of his gospel narrative?

When the wine ran out at the wedding in Cana, Jesus' mother told Him about it. He had an interesting response: "Woman, what does that have to do with us? My hour has not yet come" (John 2:4). The direct address, "woman," was respectful but instructive. Jesus was no longer under His mother's authority or compelled to act because of their close relationship. His public ministry had been inaugurated and affirmed by the Father at His baptism, and through the 40-day testing that He had recently endured.

The phrase "My hour has not yet come" enigmatically refers to His death and subsequent glorification—which would eventually issue in the establishment of the messianic Kingdom. Jesus courteously, but clearly, told His mother that her desires in this matter were not necessarily His obligation. And further, the Kingdom age that He would establish was not yet at hand.

Why is this significant? Old Testament prophecies make it clear that the messianic age would be marked by an abundance of wine, as a symbol of Israel's prosperity. Genesis 49:10-11 is a prophetic passage revealing that the Messiah would come from Judah, and His reign would be marked by this prosperity as symbolized by the abundance of wine. In the messianic age, wine will be as abundant as wash water (Gen. 49:11). Amos 9:13-14 confirms that in the Kingdom age the "mountains will drip sweet wine" and "they will also plant vineyards and drink their wine." See also Isaiah 25:6-9.

For the sake of His disciples, and out of kindness to those at the wedding, Jesus did indeed turn wash water into wine. It revealed not only His glory as God the Son, but also His glory as the promised Messiah. "This beginning of His signs Jesus did in Cana of Galilee, and manifested His glory, and His disciples believed in Him" (John 2:11).

The Messiah's reign on the earth is yet future. That promised restoration of creation is still to come (Rom. 8:18-23). When it comes, believers will be able to enjoy the fullness of Messiah's prosperous reign. Until then, Jesus' followers are ever-learning to be content in whatever circumstances they find themselves in—in abundance or in want (Phil. 4:12-13).

Jesus' miracle at the wedding in Cana should cause us to see His glory as God the Son, the promised Messiah—and cause us to long for that great Wedding Feast, which will take place when Christ's glorious Kingdom reign comes to earth.

# 4

## The Bereans—Suspicious or Submissive?

### Acts 17:10-14

10    The brethren immediately sent Paul and Silas away by night to
      Berea, and when they arrived, they went into the synagogue of the
      Jews.
11    Now these were more noble-minded than those in Thessalonica, for
      they received the word with great eagerness, examining the
      Scriptures daily to see whether these things were so.
12    Therefore many of them believed, along with a number of
      prominent Greek women and men.
13    But when the Jews of Thessalonica found out that the word of God
      had been proclaimed by Paul in Berea also, they came there as well,
      agitating and stirring up the crowds.
14    Then immediately the brethren sent Paul out to go as far as the sea;
      and Silas and Timothy remained there.

Many times we've heard the concept of being a "good Berean"
in the context of making sure that what is said from the pulpit is
actually found in the Bible. And there is an element of truth to
this.

But could it be that we've subtly embraced the idea that being a
"good Berean" is to be "wary" or "suspicious" of what is being
taught, rather than being open to change our understanding
based upon the truth revealed in the Word of God?[2]

Notice the context of Acts 17. Paul, as was his custom, went to
the Jewish synagogue in Thessalonica and gave evidence from

---

[2] Thanks to Dr. Richard Caldwell for this observation.

18

the Scripture that the Christ had to suffer and rise again from the dead—and that Jesus was the Christ (Acts 17:1-3). Because of the positive response of faith from some Jews and a massive response of faith from the God-fearing Gentiles and a number of leading women, the larger segment of the Jewish audience became hostile (Acts 17:4-5).

Out of jealousy, these Jews stirred up a mob and began a persecution of the new believers. In order to protect Paul, the fledgling church sent him away to Berea—a city 40 miles west of Thessalonica.

Acts 17:11 makes a point about the Bereans by way of contrast: *"Now these were more noble-minded than those in Thessalonica, for they received the word with great eagerness, examining the Scriptures daily to see whether these things were so"* (emphasis added). Yes, the Bereans examined the Scriptures to make sure that the teaching was in accordance with what the Word of God revealed. But the contrast and emphasis is that unlike the majority of the Jews in Thessalonica, the Bereans "received the word *with great eagerness.*"

So rather than being leery, they were eager. Rather than being suspicious of the teachers, they were submissive to the truth. They model an eagerness to change their own preconceptions and their misinformed understanding—and to conform to the Scriptures.

The religious majority in Thessalonica were steeped in their traditions and in their cultural interpretations. When confronted with the truth, they rejected it. The receptive majority in Berea were genuinely open to the truth of God's Word, even if it meant having to repent of wrong thinking, and long-held interpretations that did not actually line up with the Word of God.

19

Next time you think about being a good Berean, don't let suspicion be your guiding principle, but rather submission to the truth found in the Bible.

# 5

## Job's Repentance or Job's Rest?

### Job 42:6

1    Then Job answered the LORD and said,
2    "I know that You can do all things,
       And that no purpose of Yours can be thwarted.
3    'Who is this that hides counsel without knowledge?'
       "Therefore I have declared that which I did not understand,
       Things too wonderful for me, which I did not know."
4    'Hear, now, and I will speak;
       I will ask You, and You instruct me.'
5    "I have heard of You by the hearing of the ear;
       But now my eye sees You;
6    Therefore I retract,
       And I repent in dust and ashes."

Throughout the Book of Job, the embattled hero maintained that his suffering was *not* due to some hidden sin, as his friends and counselors had supposed. Yet at the end of the book, after God reveals Himself, Job declares, "… I *repent* in dust and ashes" (Job 42:6).

It is indeed possible to say that though sin did not cause Job's suffering, his suffering did indeed lead him to sin. But the most common meaning of Hebrew word translated "repent" in Job 42:6 may give us a different perspective on what Job was actually saying after God finally spoke to him.

The Hebrew word translated "repent" (*nhm*) is more commonly translated "consoled" or "comforted". It has at its root the idea of breathing a deep sigh. It can perhaps communicate "sorrow" or "repentance"—but most often refers to "comfort," "consolation," or less frequently "rest" after some intense experience.

It is very possible that Job was saying, "I am consoled in dust and ashes." But what about the first part of verse six— "therefore I retract"? Doesn't that communicate repentance? Note the context. In chapters 38-42, God revealed Himself, His inscrutable wisdom, and His incalculable power to Job in a way that Job had never considered or "seen" before.

Throughout the poetic portion of the book, Job had asked to cross-examine God about his suffering and make his case, using legal language. The very beginning of Job's complaint comes in chapter three, as he declared that he wished he had never been born, or that he had at least died at birth. In fact, Job 3:26 ends the chapter with this statement: "I am not at ease, nor am I quiet, and I am not at rest, but rage comes." The word "rest" is a term related to the word "repent" or "comforted". Job said, "I wish I had never been born … I have no comfort."

But after seeing God's wisdom revealed in a way he had never before considered, Job said, "I retract"—I reject my death-wish and my desire to cross-examine God, and I am consoled and at rest in dust and ashes."

In 30:19, Job had described his life as "dust and ashes" (same terms). And according to 2:8, Job had been literally sitting in ashes. But now he was no longer without comfort in his pain.

Job was still at death's door physically, still in pain, still childless and penniless, living in the town dump. His friends, family, and all those around him believed he was a wicked hypocrite. But seeing God's wisdom and power—knowing God through His revealed Word—was enough to give him rest and comfort.

Job did not curse God to His face as Satan had wagered (Job 1-2). Rather, Job demonstrated that knowing God is enough for the believer. Whatever you may face at this moment, keep seeking God—even when He seems silent. He is our only true and lasting source of comfort—even in dust and ashes.

# 6

## Jonah the Animal Rights Activist?

### Jonah 4:9-11

9    Then God said to Jonah, "Do you have good reason to be angry about the plant?" And he said, "I have good reason to be angry, even to death."

10    Then the LORD said, "You had compassion on the plant for which you did not work and which you did not cause to grow, which came up overnight and perished overnight.

11    "Should I not have compassion on Nineveh, the great city in which there are more than 120,000 persons who do not know the difference between their right and left hand, as well as many animals?"

Have you ever wondered why the Book of Jonah ends the way it ends? It seems a bit anticlimactic for God to rhetorically ask: "Should I not have compassion on Nineveh, the great city in which there are more than 120,000 persons who do not know the difference between their right and left hand …"—then finish with the phrase, "*as well as many animals*".

Why the mention of the "many animals" in Nineveh? Was God's concern for the animals equal to that of the men, women and children of Nineveh? There can be no doubt that God is concerned about the well-being of animals. Proverbs 12:10 says: "A righteous man has regard for the life of his animal …" (cf. Ps. 36:6). Jesus also spoke of God's care for the birds—*but He also emphasized that God's care for human beings exceeds that of the animal realm* (Matt. 6:26; 10:29-31; Luke 12:24).

In Jonah chapter three, the people of Nineveh repented at the preaching of Jonah, and God did not destroy the city. Thus, 4:1 reads: "But it greatly displeased Jonah and he became angry." The prophet wanted the people of Nineveh to experience the just penalty for their atrocities against God and His people. When God's mercy was extended to them, Jonah was angry.

Jonah went outside the city to observe what would happen (Jonah 4:5). Perhaps he thought their repentance would be short-lived, and thus God would then destroy them. Whatever the case, it was very hot and the "LORD God appointed a plant and it grew up over Jonah to be a shade over his head to deliver him from his discomfort. And Jonah was extremely happy about the plant" (Jonah 4:6). God had *compassion* on His disobedient prophet.

To graciously teach Jonah, however, the next day God appointed a worm to destroy the plant. And when Jonah's shade was taken away, he became angry and wanted to die (Jonah 4:7-8). God wanted Jonah to see that his concern was *his own comfort* and *his own sense of justice*. Jonah was concerned about a plant that he had nothing to do with planting, cultivating, or sustaining. It simply gave him shade. It was here and gone in a day.

God, however, is concerned about people—those created in His image. And in particular God speaks of 120,000 persons who did not know between their right and left hand—perhaps infants. Is it more righteous to be concerned about a plant (and your personal comfort) or 120,000 human beings?

Then as a final word to this book, God adds: "… as well as many animals." Could it be that the Lord ends on a note of sanctified sarcasm? If Jonah were not concerned about human beings, maybe he would be concerned about "animals". If he loved plants more than people, maybe at least he could have a little concern for the animals!

Like Jonah and Nineveh, we too are unworthy sinners who have received the merciful compassion of God. May God grant us His perspective, which produces genuine compassion for others.

# 7

## The Wilderness Temptation and Wild Beasts

### Mark 1:13

13   And He was in the wilderness forty days being tempted by Satan; and He was with the wild beasts, and the angels were ministering to Him.

Of all the Gospel accounts, only Mark records the detail that during the forty days of Jesus' wilderness temptation, "He was with the wild beasts." Why?

Each Gospel writer had a unique purpose and audience in mind as he wrote—all the while, the Spirit of God was superintending his writing. Mark's original audience was evidently familiar with Latin, as he repeatedly uses transliterated Latin terms without any translation.[3] As well, his audience was evidently not familiar with some of the Jewish practices, as he takes time to explain Jewish customs and terms that the other Gospel writers do not (i.e., Mark 7:3-4, 11).

In Mark 15:21, there is an interesting note about "Simon of Cyrene" as "the father of Alexander and Rufus." Evidently, the original audience would have been familiar with these men. The Apostle Paul mentioned "Rufus" in his epistle to the Romans (Rom. 16:13). This aligns with the testimony of early church

---

[3] Most notably 6:27 [executioner]; 6:37; 15:29, 44 [centurion—transliterated spelling used only in Mark].

historians who claim that Mark was written to persecuted believers in Rome.

Historians also report that some believers in Rome, beginning with the Neronian persecution in AD 64, were fed to ravenous dogs and burned as torches (Tacitus, Annals, 15-44). Not too many years later, other wild beasts were incorporated into the torture and murder of Christians in Rome.

Yet, according to Psalm 91:11-13, the Messiah would "tread upon the lion and cobra". In fact, Satan twisted Psalm 91:11-12 to tempt Jesus (cf. Matt. 4:6). Could it be that part of Jesus' testing in the wilderness was indeed having to trust His Father with His life in the face of the very real threat and menace of "wild beasts"?

At the heart of Mark's account stands a passage that aptly summarizes his purpose in writing. Mark 8:34-38 calls believers to follow Christ—even unto death if necessary. "If anyone wishes to come after Me, he must deny himself, and take up his cross and follow Me. For whoever wishes to save his life will lose it, but whoever loses his life for My sake and the gospel's will save it" (Mark 8:34-35).

It would seem at least plausible, if not likely, that Mark included the specific detail of Jesus with the "wild beasts" during His period of testing to encourage and strengthen His followers—some of whom would soon be facing their own test of faith before "wild beasts."

Though some even today are facing this type of persecution, many believers are not. Whatever our test, we can know that Jesus was in every way tempted as we are—yet without sin (Heb. 4:15). And because He bore the full weight of temptation, He is able to be a merciful and compassionate High Priest. Jesus knows—and He cares. "Therefore let us draw near with confidence to the throne of grace, so that we may receive mercy and find grace to help in time of need" (Heb. 4:16).

# 8

## He Shall Be Called a Nazarene

### Matthew 2:23

21  So Joseph got up, took the Child and His mother, and came into the land of Israel.

22  But when he heard that Archelaus was reigning over Judea in place of his father Herod, he was afraid to go there. Then after being warned by God in a dream, he left for the regions of Galilee,

23  and came and lived in a city called Nazareth. This was to fulfill what was spoken through the prophets: "He shall be called a Nazarene."

There is no explicit verse in the Bible that predicted that Messiah would be "called a Nazarene." So, what did Matthew mean when he wrote that Jesus and His family's move to Nazareth "was to fulfill what was spoken through the prophets: 'He shall be called a Nazarene'"?

Nazareth was a town in Galilee that was proverbial as a place of scorn. As one of Jesus' future disciples would rhetorically ask, "Can any good thing come out of Nazareth?" (John 1:46). The obvious implication was that nothing good ever comes out of Nazareth. A Nazarene was despised by his own countrymen.

There are multiple prophecies in the Scripture that the Messiah would be an object of contempt and ridicule—i.e., a Nazarene. Isaiah 49:7 reads: "Thus says the LORD … to the despised One, to the One abhorred by the nation …" (see also Ps. 22:6; Is. 9:1). Isaiah 53:3 says: "He was despised and forsaken of men, a man of sorrows and acquainted with grief; and like one from whom men hide their face He was despised, and we did not esteem Him."

As well, the previous prophetic fulfillments mentioned in Matthew chapter two seem to identify Messiah as the true Israelite, One whose life paralleled that of the nation's prophetic history (cf. Matt. 2:15, 17-18). And the Old Testament clearly identified Israel as an object of ridicule and shame to the nations around her (Gen. 43:32; Ps. 44:13-15; Is. 52:14).

Could it be that Matthew wanted his audience to be humbled by the reality that though Israel had despised this Nazarene, Jesus—they were the despised people He came to save?

If the Son of God was despised and ridiculed as a contemptible outcast—and God not only allowed it, but also providentially ordered it—why are we always striving for social acceptance and status? Why are we prone to despise others and treat them with disregard and contempt?

Jesus came to save sinners and outcasts—those who are truly contemptible before a holy God. The infinitely glorious One was despised, forsaken, and rejected—so that those who trust in Him could partake of His infinite glory.

Don't be surprised if Jesus is still disregarded today. And don't be surprised if when you follow Him in faith, you are disregarded and despised. He is Lord. He has promised that the Kingdom of Heaven belongs to such outcasts (Matt. 5:3-12).

# 9

## It's Never Too Late

### 2 Chronicles 33:10-16

10 The LORD spoke to Manasseh and his people, but they paid no attention.

11 Therefore the LORD brought the commanders of the army of the king of Assyria against them, and they captured Manasseh with hooks, bound him with bronze *chains* and took him to Babylon.

12 When he was in distress, he entreated the LORD his God and humbled himself greatly before the God of his fathers.

13 When he prayed to Him, He was moved by his entreaty and heard his supplication, and brought him again to Jerusalem to his kingdom. Then Manasseh knew that the LORD *was* God.

14 Now after this he built the outer wall of the city of David ...

15 He also removed the foreign gods and the idol from the house of the LORD, as well as all the altars which he had built on the mountain of the house of the LORD and in Jerusalem, and he threw *them* outside the city.

16 He set up the altar of the LORD and sacrificed peace offerings and thank offerings on it; and he ordered Judah to serve the LORD God of Israel.

Of all the Judean Kings in the Old Testament, far and away the most notorious was a man named Manasseh. He ruled Judah for fifty-five years (2 Chron. 33:1). Astoundingly, Manasseh was the son of one of the most godly kings in Judah's history—King Hezekiah (2 Kings 18:5).

It would seem that Manasseh set out to undo and oppose everything that his father had accomplished or intended in guiding Judah back to faith in the true God—Yahweh.

Manasseh reinstated state-sponsored idolatry. He practiced astrology, witchcraft and sorcery—employing mediums, spiritists, and diviners. He even murdered some of his own children—burning them with fire—as sacrificial offerings in his pagan worship (2 Chron. 33:2-6).

Over the years, Yahweh sent His prophets to speak to Manasseh and his people, but they paid no attention (2 Chron. 33:10). Then one day, God sovereignly intervened in Manasseh's life in a way that would forever change him. He was captured by the commanders of the Assyrian army, put in chains, and exiled in Babylon (like the disobedient nation would be approximately 50 years later).

Second Chronicles 33:11-13 records the glorious grace of God upon this chief of sinners: "... they captured Manasseh with hooks, bound him with bronze chains and took him to Babylon. When he was in distress, he entreated the LORD his God and humbled himself greatly before the God of his fathers. When he prayed to Him, He was moved by his entreaty and heard his supplication, and brought him again to Jerusalem to his kingdom. Then Manasseh knew that the LORD was God."

No doubt, Manasseh had known *about* Yahweh from his father, Hezekiah. But as an aging king in exile, held captive like an animal, Manasseh finally came to know Yahweh personally through repentance and faith.

Manasseh's faith was evidenced when God restored him to his throne. He sought to rid Jerusalem of the idolatry he once promoted. And he called others to turn from their idolatry, to worship the true and living God (2 Chron. 33:14-17).

Sadly, for the nation as a whole, a few years of reforms could not undo nearly a half a century of ardent national idolatry. After Manasseh's death, his son Amon turned back to the idolatry of his father's former years and would not humble himself as his father had (2 Chron. 33:21-23).

We learn from Manasseh's experience that the Lord is a God of grace—saving unworthy sinners, even those who had mocked Him for decades. It's never too late to repent. But though there are some "Manassehs" who come to genuine faith late in life, they will consistently testify that the consequences are high. In this life, you can't undo much of the evil that you've done. And sadly, sometimes the next generation pays little attention to the repentance of the aged.

Marvel at God's grace. Never give up hope for the lost, and never wait to repent.

# 10

## The Rivers of Eden

### Genesis 2:8-15

8    The LORD God planted a garden toward the east, in Eden; and there He placed the man whom He had formed.

9    Out of the ground the LORD God caused to grow every tree that is pleasing to the sight and good for food; the tree of life also in the midst of the garden, and the tree of the knowledge of good and evil.

10   Now a river flowed out of Eden to water the garden; and from there it divided and became four rivers.

11   The name of the first is Pishon; it flows around the whole land of Havilah, where there is gold.

12   The gold of that land is good; the bdellium and the onyx stone are there.

13   The name of the second river is Gihon; it flows around the whole land of Cush.

14   The name of the third river is Tigris; it flows east of Assyria. And the fourth river is the Euphrates.

15   Then the LORD God took the man and put him into the garden of Eden to cultivate it and keep it.

It is interesting to note that in God's description of the Garden of Eden found in Genesis 2:8-15, there are several geographical markers. First there are four rivers mention by name: the Pishon, Gihon, Tigris and Euphrates rivers. The "Tigris" and "Euphrates" are names of actual rivers today in modern-day Iraq. The "Pishon" and "Gihon" are unknown to us today, but Moses' original audience may have known their location.

Moses writes that the Pishon "flows around the whole land of Havilah, where there is gold." That "gold" is mentioned as good. Other precious stones are cited as being there as well. The "Gihon" is thought to be associated either with Africa in the region of Ethiopia, or perhaps Turkey and Armenia.

Whatever the exact location, the question remains: Why are these places and names given? Likely the worldwide flood in Noah's day changed the geography of the world dramatically.

The added note, "and from there it divided and became four rivers," could mean that the "four rivers" were tributaries that spread out within the garden—or that the garden had one river, which turned into "four rivers" once it left the garden (cf. Matthews, Vol. 1, p. 207). *Either way, it is clear that man's paradise is no myth or allegory. It was a literal, historical, geographically identifiable place.*

Genesis two is not a poetic story or fable to communicate religious tradition. The paradise of Eden was real. Man lived in a perfect world, with perfect surroundings. He lived in the midst of unspeakable beauty, unlimited provision in a historical garden in Eden. And man had *perfect fellowship with God*, who used to walk with him in that garden in the cool of the day (Gen. 3:8).

But Man was banished from the garden because of his sin (Gen. 3). The geography and climate have changed due to the flood (Gen. 6). Paradise was lost. But there remains a promised hope for man. The Seed of the woman, Who possesses the power and attributes of God, will crush the head of the one who led man into sin and death (Gen. 3:15). Revelation 21-22 describes the New Heavens and New Earth as a geographically defined place with gold and precious stones. And there is a river that sustains the new and eternal paradise of God:

> Then he showed me a river of the water of life, clear as crystal, coming from the throne of God and of the Lamb, in the middle of its street. On either side of the river was the tree of life, bearing twelve kinds of fruit, yielding its fruit every month; and the leaves of the tree were for the healing of the nations. There will no longer be any curse; and the throne

of God and of the Lamb will be in it, and His bond-servants will serve Him (Rev. 22:1-3).

There is coming a day when all those who trust in Christ will have paradise restored—literally and geographically. Fix your hope completely on that glorious day!

# 11

## Behold the Lamb of God

### Is. 53:2b, 5, 7, 10-12

2      ... He has no *stately* form or majesty
That we should look upon Him,
Nor appearance that we should be attracted to Him.

5      But He was pierced through for our transgressions,
He was crushed for our iniquities;
The chastening for our well-being *fell* upon Him,
And by His scourging we are healed.

7      He was oppressed and He was afflicted,
Yet He did not open His mouth;
Like a lamb that is led to slaughter,
And like a sheep that is silent before its shearers,
So He did not open His mouth.

10      But the LORD was pleased
To crush Him, putting *Him* to grief;
If He would render Himself *as* a guilt offering ...

11      ... My Servant, will justify the many,
As He will bear their iniquities.

12      ... He Himself bore the sin of many,
And interceded for the transgressors.

### John 1:29

29      The next day he saw Jesus coming to him and said, "Behold, the Lamb of God who takes away the sin of the world!"

Most of us have never considered the context and chronology of John the Baptist's witness to Jesus as the "Lamb of God who takes away the sin of the world" (see John 1:26-34). It would be easy to assume that this statement came the *day* after Jesus' baptism.

But notice the timing indicated in John 1:35-39:

> **35** <u>Again the next day</u> [after he had already proclaimed Jesus to be the Lamb of God] John was standing with two of his disciples,
>
> **36** and he looked at Jesus as He walked, and said, "Behold, the Lamb of God!"
>
> **37** The two disciples heard him speak, and they followed Jesus.
>
> **38** And Jesus turned and saw them following, and said to them, "What do you seek?" They said to Him, "Rabbi (which translated means Teacher), where are You staying?"
>
> **39** He said to them, "Come, and you will see." So they came and saw where He was staying; and <u>they stayed with Him that day</u>, for it was about the tenth hour.

And again in John 1:43:

> **43** <u>The next day</u> He purposed to go into Galilee, and He found Philip. And Jesus said to him, "Follow Me."

And finally John 2:1, 12:

> **1** <u>On the third day</u> there was a wedding in Cana of Galilee, and the mother of Jesus was there ...
>
> **12** <u>After this</u> He went down to Capernaum, He and His mother and *His* brothers and His disciples; and they stayed there <u>a few days</u>.

In John's account, the Baptizer identifies Jesus as the Lamb of God on two consecutive days, and Jesus stayed the second night with the two disciples. The day after that Jesus found Philip and was introduced to Nathanael. And then "three days" after that, they traveled to a wedding (John 2:1). A Jewish wedding feast could last a week. After the wedding in Cana, Jesus went to Capernaum and stayed there a few days.

But Mark 1:9-13 tells us that immediately after His baptism, Jesus went into the wilderness, and was tempted by the devil for forty days. We know from Matthew 4:1-2 that Jesus fasted for those forty days and forty nights.

It seems much more likely that Jesus was returning from His wilderness fasting and temptation, to the place where He had last left civilization. Upon seeing Jesus return from the wilderness, John called all of those gathered to "look" or "behold" the "Lamb of God who takes away the sin of the world." The prophet then bore witness that Jesus was the Son of God (John 1:30-34).

Just imagine the scene for a moment. Here was a Man coming out of the desert perhaps only after eating His first meal (administered by angels; cf. Matt. 4:11) in forty days. He may well have been emaciated, ungroomed, and more than a little in need of a change of clothes.

Even if the angels spoken of in Matthew 4:11 supplied Jesus with a change of clothes and nursed Him back to health, a solitary man coming out of the desert would have been quite an odd choice for Messiah, Son of God, King of Israel.

But perhaps that was the point. Those familiar with the Old Testament prophesies of Messiah, and His ministry as God's sacrificial lamb, would have remembered the words of Isaiah 53:2, "... *He has no stately form or majesty that we should look upon Him, nor appearance that we should be attracted to Him.*" The prophet goes on to speak of the Servant as a Lamb, and how He would render Himself a guilt offering for sinners, bear their iniquity, and justify them before God (Is. 53:1-12)—i.e., take away the sins of the world.

Certainly an unkempt, skin-and-bones Messiah would be easy to discount. Yet, God's Servant would not rely on personality, good looks, or any other superficial means to gather followers. The Word of God and the testimony of the Spirit are the tools of true ministry and true conversion.

Are you and I more influenced by a worldly perception of leadership, success, beauty, or personal charisma than the testimony of the Spirit of God through the Word of God? Our Savior had no stately form or majesty in His first coming, that men would be attracted to Him.

Yet there were those who were indeed attracted to Him. Why? He did the will of God and the works of God—and it made Him lovely in the sight of those who were enlightened by God.

Don't rely on external impressions or worldly wisdom in life and ministry. Behold, the Lamb of God and follow Him no matter what that looks like to the world.

# 12

## Why the Third Day?

### 1 Corinthians 15:3-4

3    For I delivered to you as of first importance what I also received, that Christ died for our sins according to the Scriptures,

4    and that He was buried, and that **He was raised on the third day according to the Scriptures**

### Genesis 22:1-8

1    Now it came about after these things, that God tested Abraham, and said to him, "Abraham!" And he said, "Here I am."

2    He said, "Take now your son, your only son, whom you love, Isaac, and go to the land of Moriah, and offer him there as a burnt offering on one of the mountains of which I will tell you."

3    So Abraham rose early in the morning and saddled his donkey, and took two of his young men with him and Isaac his son; and he split wood for the burnt offering, and arose and went to the place of which God had told him.

4    **On the third day** Abraham raised his eyes and saw the place from a distance.

5    Abraham said to his young men, "Stay here with the donkey, and I and the lad will go over there; and we will worship and return to you."

6    Abraham took the wood of the burnt offering and laid it on Isaac his son, and he took in his hand the fire and the knife. So the two of them walked on together.

7    Isaac spoke to Abraham his father and said, "My father!" And he said, "Here I am, my son." And he said, "Behold, the fire and the wood, but where is the lamb for the burnt offering?"

8    Abraham said, "God will provide for Himself the lamb for the burnt offering, my son." So the two of them walked on together.

### Hebrews 11:17-19

17 By faith Abraham, when he was tested, offered up Isaac, and he who had received the promises was offering up his only begotten *son;*

18 *it was he* to whom it was said, "IN ISAAC YOUR DESCENDANTS SHALL BE CALLED."

19 He considered that **God is able to raise even from the dead, from which he also received him back as a type.**

### Matthew 12:39-40

39 But He answered and said to them, "An evil and adulterous generation craves for a sign; and *yet* no sign will be given to it but the sign of Jonah the prophet;

40 for just as JONAH WAS THREE DAYS AND THREE NIGHTS IN THE BELLY OF THE SEA MONSTER, so will the Son of Man be three days and three nights in the heart of the earth.

### Hosea 6:1-2

1 "Come, let us return to the LORD.
For He has torn *us,* but He will heal us;
He has wounded *us,* but He will bandage us.

2 "He will revive us after two days;
**He will raise us up on the third day,**
**That we may live before Him.**

Have you ever wondered what passages Paul was referring to when he wrote that Christ "was raised on the third day *according to the Scriptures*" (1 Cor. 15:4)? There doesn't seem to be any explicit reference to Messiah's resurrection "*on the third day*" in the Old Testament. But perhaps upon closer examination there *are* several passages that point to the resurrection of Christ—"on the third day."

Jesus said in Matthew 12:40: "For just as JONAH WAS THREE DAYS AND THREE NIGHTS IN THE BELLY OF THE SEA MONSTER, so will the Son of Man be three days and three nights in the heart of the earth." Leaving aside the reckoning of the three days *and nights*, it is clear that Jesus was quoting from Jonah 1:17 and making the connection between Jonah's entombment in the fish and Messiah's entombment in the earth. And as Jonah's coming out of his tomb served as a sign, so would Christ's resurrection. But what was the "sign" pointing to?

According to Isaiah 49:1-6, Messiah (i.e., the Servant) is identified as Israel and yet sent to gather Israel (the nation) to Yahweh. There is a prophetic identification between Christ and the nation of Israel, yet they are distinct.

In the book of Jonah, the prophet was representative of a self-righteous Israel—who refused to fulfill their calling to be a light to the Gentile nations. Jonah would have to be entombed in the belly of the fish for three days, and then come forth alive, before he brought the message of salvation to the Gentiles. Jesus saw Jonah's three days in the fish as prophetically foreshadowing His own death for a disobedient and self-righteous people, and resurrection to life. And much like in Jonah's day—the Gentiles would first benefit.

In Hosea 6:1-2, we read that God would strike Israel for her sins, but raise her up "on the third day" that Israel might live before Him.[4] Notably, Matthew's gospel clearly connects Israel's experience as a nation, to Christ's as an individual (Matt. 2:14-15; cf. Hosea 11:1; see also Matt. 2:16-18; Jer. 31:15).

Seen in light of the prophetic solidarity between Messiah as the true Israel, and the ethnic people of Israel, Jonah 1:17 (and perhaps Hosea 6:1-2) does seem to allude to the resurrection of Christ. But there is yet an earlier reference to consider.

Genesis 22 records Abraham's test of faith and his resolve to offer his beloved son as a burnt offering as the LORD had commanded. Abraham's commitment was immediate, but the actual event happened, *"on the third day"* (Gen. 22:4). The Lord's command came on day one. Abraham, Isaac, and the

---

[4] Scholars are divided as to whether this is a superficial response on Israel's part or a call to true repentance by the prophet. Either way, it is indeed possible that the "third day" may have been recognized as having significance in God's redemptive plan. Others would argue, however, that the reference is merely poetic and has no prophetic significance.

traveling party left on day two. And they arrived at the place of Isaac's deliverance from death *on the third day*. Hebrew 11:19 makes it clear that Abraham believed that God would raise the son of promise from the dead.

As Jesus predicted His own death and resurrection "on the third day" (Matt. 16:21; 17:23; 20:19), He likely did so based upon His understanding of the Old Testament Scriptures. Genesis 22:1-8; Jonah 1:17; and perhaps Hosea 6:1-2 combine as the Scriptures that reveal the Christ would be raised "on the third day."[5]

Praise God for the detail, accuracy, yet brilliant subtlety of His Word!

---

[5] See also 2 Kings 20:3-5, 8 where Hezekiah was healed and rose from his deathbed "on the third day" according to prophecy; and Leviticus 7:15-18; 19:5-8 indicate that certain sacrifices became corrupted and unacceptable if eaten on the third day.

# 13

## Two Passover Meals?

### Luke 22:7-15

7    Then came the *first* day of Unleavened Bread on which the Passover *lamb* had to be sacrificed.

8    And Jesus sent Peter and John, saying, "Go and prepare the Passover for us, so that we may eat it."

9    They said to Him, "Where do You want us to prepare it?"

10    And He said to them, "When you have entered the city, a man will meet you carrying a pitcher of water; follow him into the house that he enters.

11    "And you shall say to the owner of the house, 'The Teacher says to you, "Where is the guest room in which I may eat the Passover with My disciples?" '

12    "And he will show you a large, furnished upper room; prepare it there."

13    And they left and found *everything* just as He had told them; and they prepared the Passover.

14    When the hour had come, He reclined *at the table,* and the apostles with Him.

15    And He said to them, "I have earnestly desired to eat this Passover with you before I suffer.

### John 18:28

28    Then they led Jesus from Caiaphas into the Praetorium, and it was early; and they themselves did not enter into the Praetorium so that they would not be defiled, but might eat the Passover.

Many Bible students have noticed a significant difficulty in reconciling the chronology of the final Passover of Jesus' ministry. Matthew, Mark, and Luke all state that the final meal Jesus ate with His disciples before His crucifixion was the

Passover meal. Yet John 18:28 seems to indicate that the Passover was the evening *after* Jesus was crucified.

Some harmonize the seeming discrepancy by claiming that John's references to "the Passover" merely speak of the Feast of Unleavened Bread, since the two became almost interchangeable in popular usage. Thus, Jesus would have been crucified the day after Passover proper.

Others harmonize the synoptic accounts with John's by postulating that there may have been two calendars in use in Jesus' day in Israel. It is supposed that the Galileans reckoned the day from sunrise-to-sunrise, while the Judeans reckoned the day from sunset-to-sunset.[6]

This would also seem to ease the strain of having to sacrifice enough lambs in one afternoon to meet the need of perhaps a quarter of a million people celebrating the festival. If this is correct, then there were two afternoons of sacrifice. Jesus ate the Passover with His disciples on Nisan 14, according to the Galilean calendar, and then was crucified on Nisan 14, according to the Judean calendar.

It is also possible that Jesus, knowing He would not be able to eat the Passover with His disciples on the next day, decided to celebrate it a day earlier in order to teach them of its genuine significance, so that after reflecting on the events of the next day, they might better understand what He had done on the cross as the divine Passover Lamb.

Though we don't know for certain which of the scenarios actually took place—or perhaps another we haven't considered—it is clear that there is more than one plausible explanation, which would reconcile the accounts.

---

[6] See the discussion in Hoehner, Harold W. *Chronological Aspects of the Life of Christ*, Grand Rapids: Zondervan 1977, pp. 74-90.

Why would God allow—even ordain—some gaps in the Bible's chronology? Hebrews 11:6 says: "And without faith it is impossible to please Him, for he who comes to God must believe that He is and that he is a rewarder of those who seek Him." He has allowed some details to remain unknown to us today, so that believers can both exercise faith and diligently seek God in His Word to understand possible ways to appropriately harmonize the accounts. These opportunities for faith become stumbling blocks to those who refuse to trust in Christ.

Praise God for the detail and clarity of His Word—and praise Him for the details we are not privy to. He is a Savior of those who trust His wisdom, His Word, and His ways.

# 14

## From Maniac to Missionary

### Mark 5:1-20

1    They came to the other side of the sea, into the country of the Gerasenes.

2    When He got out of the boat, immediately a man from the tombs with an unclean spirit met Him,

3    and he had his dwelling among the tombs. And no one was able to bind him anymore, even with a chain;

4    because he had often been bound with shackles and chains, and the chains had been torn apart by him and the shackles broken in pieces, and no one was strong enough to subdue him.

5    Constantly, night and day, he was screaming among the tombs and in the mountains, and gashing himself with stones.

6    Seeing Jesus from a distance, he ran up and bowed down before Him;

7    and shouting with a loud voice, he said, "What business do we have with each other, Jesus, Son of the Most High God? I implore You by God, do not torment me!"

8    For He had been saying to him, "Come out of the man, you unclean spirit!"

9    And He was asking him, "What is your name?" And he said to Him, "My name is Legion; for we are many."

10    And he *began* to implore Him earnestly not to send them out of the country.

11    Now there was a large herd of swine feeding nearby on the mountain.

12    *The demons* implored Him, saying, "Send us into the swine so that we may enter them."

13    Jesus gave them permission. And coming out, the unclean spirits entered the swine; and the herd rushed down the steep bank into the sea, about two thousand *of them;* and they were drowned in the sea.

14    Their herdsmen ran away and reported it in the city and in the country. And *the people* came to see what it was that had happened.

15 They came to Jesus and observed the man who had been demon-possessed sitting down, clothed and in his right mind, the very man who had had the "legion"; and they became frightened.

16 Those who had seen it described to them how it had happened to the demon-possessed man, and *all* about the swine.

17 And they began to implore Him to leave their region.

18 As He was getting into the boat, the man who had been demon-possessed was imploring Him that he might accompany Him.

19 And He did not let him, but He said to him, "Go home to your people and report to them what great things the Lord has done for you, and *how* He had mercy on you."

20 And he went away and began to proclaim in Decapolis what great things Jesus had done for him; and everyone was amazed.

### Mark 7:31; 8:1-9

**31** Again He went out from the region of Tyre, and came through Sidon to the Sea of Galilee, within the region of Decapolis.

…

**1** In those days, when there was again a large crowd and they had nothing to eat, Jesus called His disciples and said to them,

2 "I feel compassion for the people because they have remained with Me now three days and have nothing to eat.

3 "If I send them away hungry to their homes, they will faint on the way; and some of them have come from a great distance."

4 And His disciples answered Him, "Where will anyone be able *to find enough* bread here in *this* desolate place to satisfy these people?"

5 And He was asking them, "How many loaves do you have?" And they said, "Seven."

6 And He directed the people to sit down on the ground; and taking the seven loaves, He gave thanks and broke them, and started giving them to His disciples to serve to them, and they served them to the people.

7 They also had a few small fish; and after He had blessed them, He ordered these to be served as well.

8 And they ate and were satisfied; and they picked up seven large baskets full of what was left over of the broken pieces.

9 About four thousand were *there;* and He sent them away.

Many of us are familiar with the events found in the Gospels, but sometimes the geographical markers are overlooked. Yet these can provide interesting links between the narratives.

In Mark 5, Jesus healed a demonized man by freeing him from a multitude of demons. The demons subsequently destroyed an entire herd of pigs that were feeding nearby. We are told in Mark 5:1 that this happened on "the other side of the sea, into the country of the Gerasenes"—that is, on the east side of the lake commonly known as the "Sea of Galilee".

After being delivered, the former demoniac begged to accompany Jesus wherever He would go (Mark 5:18). Jesus, however, commanded the man to return to his own people and report to them what great things the Lord God had done for him, and how He had mercy on him (Mark 5:19; cf. Luke 8:39). And Mark 5:20 tells us that "he went away and began to proclaim in Decapolis what great things Jesus had done for him; and everyone was amazed."

Mark 5:21 records that Jesus crossed over again in the boat to the other side of the lake. But we read in Mark 7:31 that our Lord and His disciples once more came to the Sea of Galilee, "within the region of Decapolis," which was the same region that the delivered demoniac had gone back to testify of Christ.

As the narrative unfolds, Mark 8:1-9 records a miraculous feeding of a multitude of people—*in that same region.* In fact, Mark 8:10 uses another geographical marker to confirm that this miracle happened on the east side of the lake (see also Matt. 15:39).

Earlier in Jesus' ministry, He fed a crowd of 5000 men (Mark 6:30-44). But here we read of a slightly smaller crowd of "about four thousand" total (Mark 8:9). In the earlier feeding, there were 12 baskets of bread left over. In this feeding, there were seven. So this is clearly a different event.

Jesus had taken extended time away from the northwestern side of the lake to spend time alone with His disciples (Mark 7:24ff).

Now, on the eastern side of the lake, where Jesus did *not* spend a significant amount of time in ministry, a great crowd of people gathered in an otherwise desolate place. Why?

Just after the deliverance of the demonized man and the drowning of the pigs, those who lived in the nearby city and countryside begged Jesus to leave their region. But now, the people of this same region were bringing people to Jesus to be healed (Mark 7:32-37).

No doubt Jesus' reputation as teacher and healer preceded Him. But the geographical hints throughout Mark chapters 5-8 may well indicate that the former demoniac did indeed report the great things Jesus had done for him.

Never underestimate the impact of the testimony of one individual. God turned a maniac into a missionary. What can He do with you?

# 15

## Don't Wait Another Day

### Acts 24:22-27

22 But Felix, having a more exact knowledge about the Way, put them off, saying, "When Lysias the commander comes down, I will decide your case."

23 Then he gave orders to the centurion for him to be kept in custody and *yet* have *some* freedom, and not to prevent any of his friends from ministering to him.

**24** But some days later Felix arrived with Drusilla, his wife who was a Jewess, and sent for Paul and heard him *speak* about faith in Christ Jesus.

25 But as he was discussing righteousness, self-control and the judgment to come, Felix became frightened and said, "Go away for the present, and when I find time I will summon you."

26 At the same time too, he was hoping that money would be given him by Paul; therefore he also used to send for him quite often and converse with him.

27 But after two years had passed, Felix was succeeded by Porcius Festus, and wishing to do the Jews a favor, Felix left Paul imprisoned.

Paul likely still had the bruises and cuts from the beating he had suffered at the hands of the riotous Temple mob just five days before, when he first stood before the Roman governor Felix in Acts 24. The great Apostle must have appeared anything but great. The Jewish authorities were seeking his death, and the governor was predisposed to do them a favor. But Paul was a Roman citizen and some measure of "due process" was in order (Acts 24:22-23).

Felix's third wife, Drusilla, was a young Jewish woman who had divorced her husband to marry the governor. Little did they know, their interview with Paul would have eternal implications. No doubt Paul knew the rather scandalous circumstances of the couple's relationship as he prepared them for the good news of Christ. And such a preparation necessarily includes a discussion of "righteousness, self-control, and the judgment to come" (Acts 24:25).

Then these fateful words were recorded: "Felix became frightened and said, 'Go away for the present, and when I find time I will summon you" (Acts 24:25). Rather than responding to the frightening truths of God's righteousness, his own lack of self-control, and the sure judgment to come, Felix put off the conviction of the Holy Spirit.

After that day, there is no record of "fear" or any conviction in regard to the governor's conversations with Paul about faith in Jesus Christ. Conviction gave way to greed as he would often send for Paul and hope that money would be given him for Paul's release (Acts 24:26).

Finally, after two years of injustice, Felix's time as governor came to an end. And incredibly, he left Paul imprisoned, wishing to do the Jews a favor (Acts 24:27). In two years of conversations about Christ, Felix evidently only experienced an appropriate fear once—the first time. After that it became an intellectual and material enterprise, rather than a spiritual awakening.

We must never take the opportunity to respond to God's Word for granted. Not all moments in time are the same. A moment of conviction may come, and if not responded to, may go and never come again.[7] As messengers of the gospel, we should warn others of this same reality.

God is more gracious than we can truly comprehend. But not every moment is repeatable. Sometimes a door closes due to man's own increasingly hardened heart. The words of Hebrews 3:15 are an appropriate application of Felix's example: "Today if you hear His voice, do not harden your heart ..."

---

[7] Again, thanks to Dr. Richard Caldwell for this insight.

# 16

## Righteous Lot?

### 2 Peter 2:7-9 (cf. Gen. 13:5-13; 14:8-16; 19:1-38)

7  and *if* He rescued righteous Lot, oppressed by the sensual conduct of unprincipled men

8  (for by what he saw and heard *that* righteous man, while living among them, felt *his* righteous soul tormented day after day by *their* lawless deeds),

9  *then* the Lord knows how to rescue the godly from temptation, and to keep the unrighteous under punishment for the day of judgment

Knowing the storyline of Lot's life as recorded in the Book of Genesis, have you ever wondered why Peter calls him "righteous Lot" (2 Pet. 2:7)? According to Genesis 13:5-13, he was graciously given his choice of the land by his uncle Abram, and he chose to live *very near* Sodom—though the men of the city were exceedingly wicked and sinners against the LORD (Gen. 13:11-13).

In Genesis 14, while living *in* Sodom, Lot was caught in an international war and taken captive along with his family and all his possessions (Gen. 14:1-12). But God enabled Abram to overtake and defeat his nephew's captors, and rescue Lot, his family and all of his possessions (Gen. 14:13-16). Yet we find in Genesis 18-19 that Sodom was still exceedingly wicked, and Lot was still living among them.

The narrative of Genesis 19 contains a good measure of unflattering material as well. In a bizarre twist of hospitality,

Lot endangered his own daughters (Gen. 19:8). He was totally ineffective as a witness of God's Word (Gen. 19:14) and actually hesitated to leave the city, even though the judgment of God was about to fall (Gen. 15:15-16). He argued with God's messengers and lived in fear rather than bold faith (Gen. 19:17-20).

Perhaps the most astonishing and sickening events of Lot's life came *after* his deliverance from the destruction of Sodom. His daughters devised a plan to get their father drunk and have relations with him so as to conceive and each have a child. And they did (Gen. 19:20-38)! How then could Peter call him "righteous Lot"?

According to the Scriptures, a righteous man is one who believes God (Gen. 15:6; Rom. 3:21-22, 28; 4:5). Looking back on the Genesis narrative, you can—in hindsight—identify some evidences of Lot's faith. He did welcome and seek to protect God's messengers, putting his own life at risk (Gen. 19:1-10). He did seek to warn his sons-in-law of the impending judgment (Gen. 19:14). He did eventually leave before judgment came (Gen. 19:18-22). After leaving, Lot did not look back as the angels had instructed—though his wife did (Gen. 19:17, 26).

In the end, Peter explains: "for by what he saw and heard *that* righteous man, while living among them, felt *his* righteous soul tormented day after day by *their* lawless deeds" (2 Pet. 2:8).

It is helpful to understand the context of Peter's statement in 2 Peter two. He was reminding his readers that false teachers will come and be condemned—and many will follow them (2 Pet. 2:1-2). But God knows how to preserve and ultimately deliver those who are His (2 Pet. 2:9). Peter names two Old Testament examples to illustrate his point—Noah and Lot (2 Pet. 2:5, 7).

Noah was known as a righteous and blameless man (Gen. 6:9). Lot was known for his folly and weakness (Gen. 19). Yet to illustrate his point, the Apostle Peter chose perhaps the strongest Old Testament believer who was delivered from God's judgment on sinners, *and* the weakest believer who was just as surely delivered from God's judgment on sinners.

The true believer will never experience God's wrath. God will deliver those who trust in Him—no matter how weak or how strong!

Praise God that He is gracious and faithful to save sinners!

# 17

## Jonah's Prophecy Against Nineveh

### Jonah 3:4-10

4    Then Jonah began to go through the city one day's walk; and he cried out and said, "Yet forty days and Nineveh will be overthrown."

5    Then the people of Nineveh believed in God; and they called a fast and put on sackcloth from the greatest to the least of them.

6    When the word reached the king of Nineveh, he arose from his throne, laid aside his robe from him, covered *himself* with sackcloth and sat on the ashes.

7    He issued a proclamation and it said, "In Nineveh by the decree of the king and his nobles: Do not let man, beast, herd, or flock taste a thing. Do not let them eat or drink water.

8    "But both man and beast must be covered with sackcloth; and let men call on God earnestly that each may turn from his wicked way and from the violence which is in his hands.

9    "Who knows, God may turn and relent and withdraw His burning anger so that we will not perish."

10   When God saw their deeds, that they turned from their wicked way, then God relented concerning the calamity which He had declared He would bring upon them. And He did not do *it.*

Did Jonah's prophecy against Nineveh fail or did God fail keep His Word? Jonah 3:4 records Jonah's message: "Yet forty days and Nineveh will be overthrown." But Jonah 3:10 says: "...God relented concerning the calamity which he had declared he would bring upon them. And he did not do it."

We know from passages like Numbers 23:19 that God does not change or change His mind in an ultimate sense: "God is not a man, that He should lie, Nor a son of man, that He should

59

repent; Has He said, and will He not do it? Or has He spoken, and will He not make it good?" (cf. 1 Samuel 15:29).

Some explain this difficult passage by pointing to the anthropomorphic language—that human terms are used of God to help us understand God in ways that our finite mind can comprehend. Others rightly point out that God's promises of judgment are always conditional. As it says in Jeremiah 18:7-8: "At one moment I might speak concerning a nation or concerning a kingdom to uproot, to pull down, or to destroy it; if that nation against which I have spoken turns from its evil, I will relent concerning the calamity I planned to bring on it."

But perhaps here in Jonah, the language itself reveals that Jonah's prophecy actually did come to pass. The Hebrew word for "overthrown" means literally, "turned" or "turned over". It can certainly imply destruction (Gen. 19:25, 29), but it can also speak of being "changed" (Ex. 7:15; Deut. 23:5; 1 Sam. 10:6, 9; Est. 9:1, 22; Ps. 41:3).

Jonah employed a word that can mean either destroyed or changed. "Yet forty days and Nineveh will be changed." And that's exactly what happened. Nineveh did repent and truly was changed by faith.

Did God "change" His mind, however? The word translated "relented" (or as some translations render it, "repented" or "changed His mind") is not the word "turn". It comes from the Hebrew root *nhm*, which means, "be consoled", or "to be moved to compassion".

Jonah's prophecy came to pass, and God did not change His course. Instead, Nineveh was truly changed, and God was consoled concerning their destruction. He takes no pleasure in the destruction of the wicked (Ez. 33:11-19). He finds consolation in the repentance of sinners.

Isaiah 55:7 is an appropriate exhortation in light of the example of God's dealings with Nineveh in Jonah's day: "Let the wicked forsake his way and the unrighteous man his thoughts, and let him return to the LORD, and he will have compassion on him, and to our God, for He will abundantly pardon."

# 18

## Peter's Faithless Denials and Peter's Faithful Death

### John 18:17, 25-27

17    Then the slave-girl who kept the door said to Peter, "You are not also *one* of this man's disciples, are you?" He said, "I am not."

     ...

25    Now Simon Peter was standing and warming himself. So they said to him, "You are not also *one* of His disciples, are you?" He denied *it*, and said, "I am not."

26    One of the slaves of the high priest, being a relative of the one whose ear Peter cut off, said, "Did I not see you in the garden with Him?"

27    Peter then denied *it* again, and immediately a rooster crowed.

### John 21:15-19

15    So when they had finished breakfast, Jesus said to Simon Peter, "Simon, *son* of John, do you love Me more than these?" He said to Him, "Yes, Lord; You know that I love You." He said to him, "Tend My lambs."

16    He said to him again a second time, "Simon, *son* of John, do you love Me?" He said to Him, "Yes, Lord; You know that I love You." He said to him, "Shepherd My sheep."

17    He said to him the third time, "Simon, *son* of John, do you love Me?" Peter was grieved because He said to him the third time, "Do you love Me?" And he said to Him, "Lord, You know all things; You know that I love You." Jesus said to him, "Tend My sheep.

18    "Truly, truly, I say to you, when you were younger, you used to gird yourself and walk wherever you wished; but when you grow old, you will stretch out your hands and someone else will gird you, and bring you where you do not wish to *go*."

19    Now this He said, signifying by what kind of death he would glorify God. And when He had spoken this, He said to him, "Follow Me!"

Many have seen the parallels between Peter's faithless denials and the thrice repeated question, "Simon, son of John, do you love Me?" when our resurrected Lord Jesus restored Peter on the shore of the Sea of Galilee. But perhaps we haven't seen the connection between Peter's final answer and Jesus' prediction of Peter's death.

Jesus' first two questions employed the Greek term *agapao*—which speaks of the love of the highest commitment and fidelity. Both times Peter answered using a different term—*phileo* (a love characterized by affection; deep brotherly affection). But the third time Jesus asked, "Simon, son of John, do you love Me?" Jesus also used the term *phileo*. Simon, son of John, you have said you really have a deep brotherly affection for Me—but do you?[8]

This final question grieved Peter, because it was the third time, and perhaps Jesus now even questions Peter's current assessment. The denials had revealed that Peter's love was not what he had thought it was (cf. Matt. 26:35). But Peter knew the deep affection he felt for his Master. So he appealed to the One who knew everything to verify what was in his heart: "Lord, You know all things; You know that I love (*phileo*) You." To this, Jesus simply replied much as He had the two times previous: "Tend My sheep."

If the narrative ended there, Peter might have been left with the impression that the final assessment of his love would be

---

[8] Many scholars regard the interplay of *agapao* and *phileo* as merely stylistic, much like the different but synonymous terms "sheep" and "lambs, as well as "shepherd" and 'tend" in this same context. But clearly the translators did want to make a distinction in that they used different words for "shepherd" and "tend" as well as "lambs" and "sheep". There are indeed nuances in those different terms, but in English, "love" is the word that translates both *agapao* and *phileo*. No doubt they are synonyms, but the nuances may be emphasized here because Jesus actually changes words for His final question, while Peter does not change terms. Even if the change is merely stylistic, the point of Peter's restoration and confirmation of his love is found in Jesus' prophecy of his death that follows.

determined by *his* faithfulness to tend Christ's sheep. And based upon his recent past performance, that could not have been very encouraging. But Jesus didn't stop there.

Our Lord went on to encourage Peter by revealing that he would be faithful and demonstrate a love of the highest commitment and fidelity in regard to Christ. In essence, Jesus said: "I know you will find this difficult to believe right now, but it's true. When you were younger you determined the course of your life, but when you are old you will indeed glorify Me by dying a martyr's death" (cf. John 21:18-19).

Though the Son of God Himself promised Peter's fidelity even unto death, He called Peter to exercise his human responsibility by saying, "Follow Me!"

Genuine love for Christ is dependent upon His grace, not on our ability to love Him. But those who love the Lord are responsible to follow Him wherever He leads.

# 19

## Gideon's Fleece—Personal or Corporate Assurance?

### Judges 6:33-7:1

33    Then all the Midianites and the Amalekites and the sons of the east assembled themselves; and they crossed over and camped in the valley of Jezreel.

34    So the Spirit of the LORD came upon Gideon; and he blew a trumpet, and the Abiezrites were called together to follow him.

35    He sent messengers throughout Manasseh, and they also were called together to follow him; and he sent messengers to Asher, Zebulun, and Naphtali, and they came up to meet them.

36    Then Gideon said to God, "If You will deliver Israel through me, as You have spoken,

37    behold, I will put a fleece of wool on the threshing floor. If there is dew on the fleece only, and it is dry on all the ground, then I will know that You will deliver Israel through me, as You have spoken."

38    And it was so. When he arose early the next morning and squeezed the fleece, he drained the dew from the fleece, a bowl full of water.

39    Then Gideon said to God, "Do not let Your anger burn against me that I may speak once more; please let me make a test once more with the fleece, let it now be dry only on the fleece, and let there be dew on all the ground."

40    God did so that night; for it was dry only on the fleece, and dew was on all the ground.

1    Then Jerubbaal (that is, Gideon) and all the people who were with him, rose early and camped beside the spring of Harod …

The story of Gideon and the sign of the fleece is familiar to many. Some have taken it as a proof text to justify asking God for a sign to determine His will for one's personal decisions.

Others have taken Gideon to task for being extremely weak in his faith, needing two signs to prompt him to obey God's call.

There are, however, clues in the text that may lead us to a different understanding of Gideon's requests concerning the sign of the fleece. Judges 6:34-35 indicates that Gideon's request concerning the fleece came after 32,000 men had rallied around him to fight the Midianites (cf. 7:3 for the accounting of the 32,000).

Notably, the LORD had already told Gideon in 6:16 that he would "defeat Midian as one man." At that time, Gideon did seek verification that it was indeed Yahweh who was speaking with him (the sign being the miraculous acceptance of Gideon's offering—see 6:17-22). But the fleece sign was requested while Gideon was surrounded by an army of 32,000 that he had called together.

Could it be that Gideon's request concerning the fleece was not merely for personal assurance as his faith wavered? Could it be that he desired to offer assurance to this army that the LORD had indeed called him to lead Israel in battle against the Midianites? Moreover, perhaps the second request—dry fleece with wet ground—came upon the reasoning of many who might assume that the first sign was a natural phenomenon (6:36-40).

If this is the case, Gideon's faith was not as weak as some may have assumed, but rather he was seeking corporate assurance for the army that would follow him into battle. But, the question remains, why the final sign in 7:9-11?

> Now the same night it came about that the LORD said to him, "Arise, go down against the camp, for I have given it into your hands. But if you are afraid to go down, go with Purah your servant down to the camp, and you will hear what they say; and afterward your hands will be strengthened that you may go down against the camp."

At that point, God had reduced Gideon's army down from 32,000 men to only 300. Most of us would struggle with the prospect of facing a vast opposing army with only 300 men. It would seem that Gideon did indeed need encouragement. But interestingly, the LORD told him to take along Purah, Gideon's servant, along to hear the enemy's dream and its interpretation. Purah could verify to the 300 soldiers that God had again verified that Gideon's band of 300 would be victorious.

The Gideon narrative is descriptive—not prescriptive. It does not call us to ask for signs to verify God's will. We have the written Word of God—much more revelation than Gideon had. The LORD may, however, at times grant clear confirmation of a particular application of His will in our lives. Moreover, it may be appropriate at times to ask that He bring assurance to those we lead.

Whatever our assessment of Gideon's faith in requesting a sign, we should remember that King Yahweh is the real leader of His people. He uses earthen vessels to display His heavenly glory. The LORD's defeat of tens of thousands through Gideon and 300 men is a testimony to God's grace, God's power, and God's wisdom.

Let us, therefore, press on in faith, offering our allegiance to the One who is God's grace, God's power, and God's wisdom incarnate—Jesus Christ.

# 20

## Samson's Revenge or Repentance?

### Hebrews 11:32-34

32   And what more shall I say? For time will fail me if I tell of Gideon, Barak, Samson, Jephthah, of David and Samuel and the prophets,

33   who by faith conquered kingdoms, performed *acts of* righteousness, obtained promises, shut the mouths of lions,

34   quenched the power of fire, escaped the edge of the sword, from weakness were made strong, became mighty in war, put foreign armies to flight.

### Judges 14:1-3, 7

1   Then Samson went down to Timnah and *saw* a woman in Timnah, one of the daughters of the Philistines (emphasis added).

2   So he came back and told his father and mother, "I *saw* a woman in Timnah, *one* of the daughters of the Philistines; now therefore, get her for me as a wife."

3   Then his father and his mother said to him, "Is there no woman among the daughters of your relatives, or among all our people, that you go to take a wife from the uncircumcised Philistines?" But Samson said to his father, "Get her for me, for she *looks* good to me [literally, "she is right in my eyes]"
    ...

7   So he went down and talked to the woman; and she *looked* good to Samson [literally, "was right in Samson's eyes].

### Judges 16:1, 4, 18, 20-21, 28

1   Now Samson went to Gaza and *saw* a harlot there, and went in to her (emphasis added).

4   After this it came about that he loved a woman in the valley of Sorek, whose name was Delilah.

18    When Delilah saw that he had told her all *that was* in his heart, she sent and called the lords of the Philistines, saying, "Come up once more, for he has told me all *that is* in his heart." Then the lords of the Philistines came up to her and brought the money in their hands.

20    She said, "The Philistines are upon you, Samson!" And he awoke from his sleep and said, "I will go out as at other times and shake myself free." But he did not know that the LORD had departed from him.

21    Then the Philistines seized him and gouged out his eyes; and they brought him down to Gaza and bound him with bronze chains, and he was a grinder in the prison.

28    Then Samson called to the LORD and said, "O Lord GOD, please remember me and please strengthen me just this time, O God, that I may at once be avenged of the Philistines for my two eyes."

### Judges 17:6

6    In those days there was no king in Israel; every man did what was right in his own eyes.

### Judges 21:25

25    In those days there was no king in Israel; everyone did what was right in his own eyes.

Samson's inclusion in Hebrews 11 has perplexed many. A casual read of Judges 13-16, may seem to depict him as an immoral, selfish, vindictive man.[9]

It should be noted, however, that Samson judged Israel for 20 years (Judges 15:20), and the events recorded do not cover all of those years in detail. They do, however, offer glimpses of his character at various times during those years—and the picture is admittedly less than flawless.

A key to understanding the purpose of the narrative in Judges is seeing the theme of the book as repeated in 17:6 and 21:25: "In those days there was no king in Israel; *everyone did what was right in his own eyes*." Yahweh was Israel's rightful King, but

---

[9] For a very different assessment of Samson's life and ministry see Daniel Arnold's excellent book, *Judges: Mysterious Heroes of the Faith*, pp. 267-335.

in her disobedience, Israel had, for all practical purposes, rejected Him (cf. Judges 8:23; 1 Sam. 8:7; 10:19; 12:12).

Samson was a true representative of his generation. He too seemingly did what was right in his own eyes (cf. 14:3, 7 for the same expression). What he "saw," he pursued (cf. 14:1; 16:1).

We can see glimmers of faith in that he evidently believed, to some extent, the witness of his mother and father to Yahweh as recorded in chapter 13. After all, he never did cut his hair (cf. 16:17). In 15:18-29, Samson prayed to Yahweh for help, and Yahweh helped him miraculously.

But when he was finally captured, his eyes literally gouged out, Samson most clearly expressed his faith and spiritual vision, as 16:28 reads: "Then Samson called to the LORD and said, "O Lord GOD, please remember me and please strengthen me just this time, O God ..." He used the covenant name Yahweh. He addressed God as *Adonai*—Sovereign Master. And he used the word *Elohim*, which refers to Yahweh's power as *God of gods*.

Samson clearly knew that the LORD alone was the source of strength. Yet, as his prayer continued he said: "... that I may at once be avenged of the Philistines for my two eyes" (some versions read: "if only for one of my two eyes"). Was this a final prayer of faith mixed with a prayer of selfish revenge for the loss of his eyes?

Since the previous account seems to so unabashedly record his sinful flaws, a desire for personal revenge may have been present. But could it be that Samson was actually expressing sorrow over living so frequently by sight rather than by faith (see Judges 14:1-3, 7 [v. 3, 7 literally say: 'right in my eyes']; 16:1, 4, 18)? The Hebrew could be plainly rendered: "And let me take revenge with a singular vengeance—because of my two eyes—from the Philistines." [10]

---

[10] Block, D. I. (1999). *Judges, Ruth* (Vol. 6). Nashville: Broadman & Holman Publishers. Though Dr. Block would likely not see any reference to repentance here.

Could it be that Samson was acknowledging that his death and the destruction of the Philistines in the temple would only be a partial vindication of the wrongs perpetrated, *because of his eyes*?

Though we cannot be sure of the motive behind Samson's final prayer, we can be sure he prayed in faith to the true God—the only source of strength.

Samson's life and death help us to see that God chooses to use sinners with faith—however flawed they may be. He was a man of faith and apparently great faults. His life and death call us to seek God's help to turn away from doing what is right in our own eyes, and to live life by faith in submission to the true King.

# 21

## Ahithophel

### 2 Samuel 16:20-23 (cf. 2 Sam. 11:3; 23:34)

20   Then Absalom said to Ahithophel, "Give your advice. What shall we do?"

21   Ahithophel said to Absalom, "Go in to your father's concubines, whom he has left to keep the house; then all Israel will hear that you have made yourself odious to your father. The hands of all who are with you will also be strengthened."

22   So they pitched a tent for Absalom on the roof, and Absalom went in to his father's concubines in the sight of all Israel.

23   The advice of Ahithophel, which he gave in those days, *was* as if one inquired of the word of God; so was all the advice of Ahithophel *regarded* by both David and Absalom.

### 2 Samuel 17:1-5, 14, 23

1   Furthermore, Ahithophel said to Absalom, "Please let me choose 12,000 men that I may arise and pursue David tonight.

2   "I will come upon him while he is weary and exhausted and terrify him, so that all the people who are with him will flee. Then I will strike down the king alone,

3   and I will bring back all the people to you. The return of everyone depends on the man you seek; *then* all the people will be at peace."

4   So the plan pleased Absalom and all the elders of Israel.

5   Then Absalom said, "Now call Hushai the Archite also, and let us hear what he has to say."

14   Then Absalom and all the men of Israel said, "The counsel of Hushai the Archite is better than the counsel of Ahithophel." For the LORD had ordained to thwart the good counsel of Ahithophel, so that the LORD might bring calamity on Absalom.

23   Now when Ahithophel saw that his counsel was not followed, he saddled *his* donkey and arose and went to his home, to his city, and

set his house in order, and strangled himself; thus he died and was buried in the grave of his father.

Ahithophel was a trusted advisor to King David until he betrayed the king to become the lead counselor for David's son Absalom. It is thought that David had Ahithophel in mind when he penned Psalm 41:9: "Even my close friend in whom I trusted, who ate my bread, has lifted up his heel against me" (quoted by Jesus in John 13:18 as being ultimately fulfilled by Judas Iscariot).

Second Samuel 16:23 testifies to Ahithophel's wisdom: "The advice of Ahithophel, which he gave in those days, *was* as if one inquired of the word of God; so was all the advice of Ahithophel *regarded* by both David and Absalom." But why would Ahithophel advise Absalom to pursue a course of sexual immorality in regard to his father's concubines? Such is not godly advice. But it would declare to Israel that Absalom had no regard for his father—and no regard for marital morality.

It is helpful to note a connection that is made elsewhere in the biblical record. Second Samuel 15:12 calls Ahithophel "the Gilonite". Second Samuel 23 records a list of David's mighty men. And mention is made in 23:34 of "Eliam the son of Ahithophel the Gilonite". So here we find that Ahithophel had a son named "Eliam" who was renowned for his military prowess as one of David's 30 elite fighters.

Previously, however, 2 Samuel 11 had recorded David's sexual sin with Bathsheba, which started with a gaze on a roof top. As it says in 2 Samuel 11:3: "So David sent and inquired about the woman. And one said, 'Is this not Bathsheba, *the daughter of Eliam*, the wife of Uriah the Hittite?'" (emphasis added).

It would appear that Ahithophel may have been the grandfather of Bathsheba. If so, David had committed sexual immorality with his granddaughter—beginning with an inappropriate look *on a roof top*. Years later, Ahithophel would counsel David's son Absalom to commit sexual immorality on David's rooftop (2 Sam. 16:20-23; cf. 12:10-12). Public disgrace would be met with public disgrace—and more.

Though God had forgiven David (cf. Ps. 32; 51), it would seem that Ahithophel had not. As wise as he was, Ahithophel sought to kill God's anointed king (cf. 2 Sam. 17:1-2). Ultimately God overturned Ahithophel's counsel: "Then Absalom and all the men of Israel said, 'The counsel of Hushai the Archite is better than the counsel of Ahithophel.' For the LORD had ordained to thwart the good counsel of Ahithophel, so that the LORD might bring calamity on Absalom" (2 Sam. 17:14).

Much like Judas would betray David's greater Son, Ahithophel betrayed David. And like Judas, Ahithophel's sin led to him to take his own life (2 Sam. 17:23).

David's sin had been covered and forgiven, but it had devastating temporal consequences. Yet Ahithophel was responsible for his own choices. In seeking David's life, he revealed a heart that was not given over to Yahweh. His selfish motives led to a selfish end.

Praise God for His revelation (even the genealogies!), His grace, His providence, and His promises to keep His own! But be prepared for difficulties and dangers in this life. How we respond makes all the difference.[11] Humility and trust are God's anchors for the forgiven sinner. Bitterness and betrayal always end in death.

---

[11] See 2 Corinthians 2:7-11 for the issue of a lack of forgiveness as a scheme of Satan.

# 22

## Ask, Seek, Knock

### Matthew 7:7-11

7   "Ask, and it will be given to you; seek, and you will find; knock, and it will be opened to you.

8   "For everyone who asks receives, and he who seeks finds, and to him who knocks it will be opened.

9   "Or what man is there among you who, when his son asks for a loaf, will give him a stone?

10   "Or if he asks for a fish, he will not give him a snake, will he?

11   "If you then, being evil, know how to give good gifts to your children, how much more will your Father who is in heaven give what is good to those who ask Him!"

### Luke 11:9-13

9   "So I say to you, ask, and it will be given to you; seek, and you will find; knock, and it will be opened to you.

10   "For everyone who asks, receives; and he who seeks, finds; and to him who knocks, it will be opened.

11   "Now suppose one of you fathers is asked by his son for a fish; he will not give him a snake instead of a fish, will he?

12   "Or if he is asked for an egg, he will not give him a scorpion, will he?

13   "If you then, being evil, know how to give good gifts to your children, how much more will *your* heavenly Father give the Holy Spirit to those who ask Him?"

It is clear from the Scriptures that God answers prayer—sometimes very specifically (Gen. 25: 21; Judges 13:8; 1 Sam. 1:11, 27; 2 Kings 19:14-20; 20:1-7; 22:19; Acts 12:5-17; cf. James 5:16-18). Moreover, most of us are familiar with Jesus' promise: "Ask, and it will be given to you; seek, and you will find ..." But many are not as familiar with the context in which it was originally given.

In Matthew seven, Jesus was calling His disciples to help one another in a spirit of humility rather than condemn one another (Matt. 7:1-5). First, we are called to take the log out of our own eye in order to be able to see clearly to be able to take the speck out of a brother's eye. Then Jesus says: "Do not give what is holy to dogs, and do not throw your pearls before swine, or they will trample them under their feet, and turn and tear you to pieces" (Matt. 7:6).

In other words, after you've humbly looked to yourself, and you genuinely want to help someone else with their sin, you need to make sure you are dealing with a believer. "Dogs" and "swine" were unclean animals that represented unbelievers. You can't deal with unbelievers in their sin in the same way you would deal with a believer.

How do you know how to deal with a brother's speck, or even know if the one you're dealing with is spiritually able to receive your help? In this context Jesus said: "Ask, and it will be given to you; seek, and you will find; knock, and it will be opened to you ..." Our Lord was promising that if you really want to know how best to help someone with their sin, then keep asking God for wisdom and He will provide that wisdom.

Jesus made a very similar statement about asking and receiving in Luke 11:9-13, but in a much broader context of instruction on prayer in general, and persistence in making the request. As well, He gave a much more specific word concerning *how* God will answer.

In Matthew 7:11, our Lord said that God would give what is "good" to those who ask. In Luke 11:13 He said: "If you then, being evil, know how to give good gifts to your children, how much more will your heavenly Father give *the Holy Spirit* to those who ask Him?" (emphasis added).

In Luke's context, Jesus had just given a model prayer, which ends with the famous petitions: "… forgive us our sins, for we ourselves also forgive everyone who is indebted to us. And lead us not into temptation" (Luke 11:4). He then gives an illustration meant to remind us that God's goodness far surpasses that of man's—so ask (Luke 11:5-13). He finishes His instruction on prayer by essentially saying "your heavenly Father [will] give the Holy Spirit to those who ask Him".

The Holy Spirit is the One who enables our forgiveness of others and our deliverance from temptation. As He produces His fruit in us, we are transformed. And this divinely wrought character—Christlikeness—is the real and lasting answer to our every request.

*The call to ask, seek, and knock is not for the sake of worldly advancement or merely personal enrichment, but for what is truly best—particularly for godly wisdom and spiritual growth.* So ask, seek, and knock in every situation. As you do, expect to see the Father make you more like Christ by the power of His Holy Spirit.

# 23

## The Chariot[s] of Israel and Its Horsemen[12]

### 2 Kings 2:11-12

11    As they were going along and talking, behold, *there appeared* a chariot of fire and horses of fire which separated the two of them. And Elijah went up by a whirlwind to heaven.

12    Elisha saw *it* and cried out, "My father, my father, the chariots of Israel and its horsemen!" And he saw Elijah no more.

### 2 Kings 13:14

14    When Elisha became sick with the illness of which he was to die, Joash the king of Israel came down to him and wept over him and said, "My father, my father, the chariots of Israel and its horsemen!"

Children's books and cartoons often depict Elijah being taken to heaven in "a chariot of fire". But a closer look at the text of 2 Kings two reveals that "Elijah went up *by a whirlwind* to heaven" (2 Kings 2:11). The "chariot of fire and horses of fire" were evidently a dispatch of the LORD's heavenly host sent to protect and accompany Elijah to glory (cf. 2 Kings 6:16-17)—but they were not the actual transport.

As Elisha saw his master Elijah taken into heaven, he cried: "My father, my father, the chariots of Israel and its horsemen!" It might be easily assumed that he was speaking of what he saw. But his words are a declaration of Elijah's ministry as prophet.

---

[12] See William Varner's excellent book on this: *The Chariot of Israel*, Friends of Israel Gospel Ministry, 1984.

Elisha spoke of his mentor as "my father". Elijah had been a spiritual father to Elisha for some time (1 Kings 19:19-21). Now he was leaving this world in a spectacular, but very permanent way. It is important to note that the Hebrew word for "chariot" in 2 Kings 2:12 is singular (cf. KJV).

Leaving this passage for a moment, we move to 2 Kings 13:14, and words spoken about Elisha's departure from this world. Though he *would* experience death—something Elijah did not—it is striking to see what was said as he was leaving this world. "When Elisha became sick with the illness of which he was to die, Joash the king of Israel came down to him and wept over him and said, 'My father, my father, the chariot [singular] of Israel, and its horsemen!" The same exact language is used.

In ancient Israel, kings and nations measured their national security in terms of "chariots and its horsemen". They combined to serve as the elite forces for national defense.

As Elisha saw Elijah taken to heaven, he was crying out that the aged prophet had been Israel's defense. The Word of God that came through the prophet of God was the very protection of God for His people. At Elisha's death, Joash declared the same thing. What was going to happen to God's people if God's prophet was no longer with them?

Notably, in view of Joash's humble acknowledgement of God's sovereign protection, through God's prophet, the LORD led Elisha to pronounce a measured, but very real assurance of Israel's defeat of Aram under Joash's rule (2 Kings 13:15-19).

God's Word must be our trust and defense as believers. Isaiah 31:1 goes so far as to actually condemn those who look to nations and military might for their hope and defense: "Woe to those who go down to Egypt for help, who rely on horses, who trust in the multitude of their chariots and in the great strength of their horsemen, but do not look to the Holy One of Israel, or seek help from the LORD."

Do we see the Word of God as our defense? Or do we look to our savings account, our right to bear arms, our job, etc.? "Some boast in chariots and some in horses, But we will boast in the name of the LORD, our God" (Psalm 20:7).

# 24

## A King, a Prophet, a Prophecy, and a Boy

### Isaiah 7:2-4, 10-16

2    When it was reported to the house of David, saying, "The Arameans have camped in Ephraim," his heart and the hearts of his people shook as the trees of the forest shake with the wind.

3    Then the LORD said to Isaiah, "Go out now to meet Ahaz, **you and your son Shear-jashub**, at the end of the conduit of the upper pool, on the highway to the fuller's field,

4    and say to him, 'Take care and be calm, have no fear and do not be fainthearted because of these two stubs of smoldering firebrands, on account of the fierce anger of Rezin and Aram and the son of Remaliah.

10    Then the LORD spoke again to Ahaz, saying,

11    "Ask a sign for yourself from the LORD your God; make *it* deep as Sheol or high as heaven."

12    But Ahaz said, "I will not ask, nor will I test the LORD!"

13    Then he said, "Listen now, O house of David! Is it too slight a thing for you to try the patience of men, that you will try the patience of my God as well?

14    "Therefore the Lord Himself will give you a sign: Behold, a virgin will be with child and bear a son, and she will call His name Immanuel.

15    "He will eat curds and honey at the time He knows *enough* to refuse evil and choose good.

16    "For before **the boy** will know *enough* to refuse evil and choose good, the land whose two kings you dread will be forsaken.

Many a Bible student has wrestled with the near and far implications the prophecy in Isaiah 7:14-16. There is unanimity among believing scholars that the ultimate fulfillment of the prophecy found in 7:14 is the birth of Jesus Christ. But there is still debate about the initial implications of the prophecy in Isaiah's day.

Isaiah 7:16 prophesied: "For before the boy will know enough to refuse evil and choose good, the land whose two kings you dread will be forsaken." In other words, within a few years the both Syria and Israel (the northern Kingdom who allied with Syria) would no longer be a threat to Ahaz and his nation, Judah.[13]

Many explain the difficulties between a near and far fulfillment by postulating there would be a young girl who would get married, conceive, have a son and name him "Immanuel". Perhaps this might be a possible explanation for the near fulfillment, but then it seems to unwittingly cast doubt on an actual "virgin" conception in the case of Christ.

A more natural understanding comes as we consider the scene of the confrontation as revealed in the context of Isaiah seven. The prophet Isaiah was commanded by the LORD to bring his young son with him to confront Ahaz (7:3). The boy's name was "Shear-Jashub," which means "a remnant will return". This may have been meant to give an added prophetic assurance to Ahab.

The prophecy in verses 14-15 of a virgin-born child who would be "God with us" served to confirm to Ahaz and Israel that the "seed promise" of Genesis 3:15, which is connected to the Davidic covenant (1 Chron. 17), would still come to pass. But what about the prophecy in verse 16? How can Jesus fulfill verses 14-15—but "the boy" of verse 16 somehow must fulfill a prophecy in Ahaz's lifetime?

Could it be that "the boy" referenced in 7:16 was not Immanuel, spoken of in 7:14-15—but rather "the boy" Shear-Jashub who had accompanied Isaiah? Before this young boy came to adulthood, the Aram-Israel alliance would be abandoned, and

---

[13] Some see this language as actually condemning Ahaz rather than a word that could comfort (Smith, Gary V. *The New American Commentary: Isaiah 1-29*; Broadman, Logos). But he agrees that "the boy" in 7:16 refers not to Immanuel of 7:14, but rather to Shear-jashub (Isaiah's young son who accompanied him to this meeting with Ahaz).

Assyria would actually take over their land. As Henry Bultema writes:

> We can imagine the prophet pointing with his finger at Shear-jashub, the little fellow he held by the hand. Before the lad would come to the years of discretion, the lands of Syria and Ephraim, before whose kings Ahaz trembles will be destroyed. The subsequent history has proven the literal fulfillment of this prophecy. Tiglath-pileser, whose aid Ahaz bought with the temple treasure, conquered Syria, killed Rezin and carried the nation's inhabitants as captives to Assyria (II Kings 16:9). This same king also took possession of the northern part of Israel and carried a great multitude of the people of the land captive to Assyria. See II Kings 15:29 and 1 Chronicles 5:36.[14]

Such an understanding preserves the integrity of the virgin birth of Christ and gives a clear sign to Ahaz.

Praise the One who is Immanuel—whose Word never fails and whose promises always come to pass!

---

[14] Bultema, Harry, *Commentary on Isaiah*, Kregel, p. 108.

# 25

## Barnabas's Cousin Mark

### Colossians 4:10

10    Aristarchus, my fellow prisoner, sends you his greetings; and *also* Barnabas's cousin Mark (about whom you received instructions; if he comes to you, welcome him).

### 2 Timothy 4:10-11

10    for Demas, having loved this present world, has deserted me and gone to Thessalonica; Crescens *has gone* to Galatia, Titus to Dalmatia.

11    Only Luke is with me. Pick up Mark and bring him with you, for he is useful to me for service.

Many remember the "sharp disagreement" that led to Paul and Barnabas's split in Acts 15:36-40. The two leading missionary-evangelists were poised to begin their second missionary journey, in which they had planned to visit and strengthen the churches God had planted through them on their first tour. However, a division arose as to whether to take Mark or not.

According to Acts 13:13, Mark returned to Jerusalem in the middle of their first missionary journey. Barnabas wanted to take Mark along with them on the second trip, "But Paul kept insisting that they should not" because he "had deserted them in Pamphylia and had not gone with them to the work" (Acts 15:38). The disagreement was not resolved, and Paul and Barnabas parted ways. "Barnabas took Mark with him and sailed away to Cyprus" and "Paul chose Silas and left" for the planned trip—with the sending church's blessing (Acts 15:40).

Notably, Acts 4:36 says that Barnabas's given name was Joseph, but that the apostles nicknamed him "Barnabas," which means "son of encouragement"—and that Barnabas was originally from Cyprus. It is also interesting that the early portion of the first missionary journey was in Cyprus (Acts 13:4).

Chronologically, the split between Paul and Barnabas happened around AD 50. After that, we hear nothing about Barnabas or Mark until their mention in Colossians 4:10: "Aristarchus, my fellow prisoner, sends you his greetings; and *also* Barnabas's cousin Mark (about whom you received instructions; if he comes to you, welcome him)."[15] The Book of Colossians was written around AD 60.

Evidently, in those ten years, Paul, Barnabas, and Mark reconciled. Barnabas was known to the Colossians, and Paul mentions Mark not only as Barnabas's cousin (possibly nephew), but also that Mark was to be welcomed by the church in Colossae. In Philemon 24, written at approximately the same time as Colossians, Paul called Mark one of his "fellow-workers."

Even more telling is the reference to Mark in the final chapter of the final letter of Paul's life. "Only Luke is with me. Pick up Mark and bring him with you, for he is useful to me for service" (2 Tim. 4:11). Paul once knew Mark as a deserter. But by the end of his life, Paul had seen the evidence of Mark's faithfulness in ministry.

As well, Mark seems to have been useful in the Apostle Peter's ministry, as Peter wrote: "She who is in Babylon, chosen together with you, sends you greetings, and so does my son, Mark" (1 Pet. 5:10). Early church tradition cites Mark as the author of Peter's account of the gospel, which we commonly refer to as the Gospel of Mark.

---

[15] Galatians 2:13 may have preceded the Jerusalem council and the split between Paul and Barnabas.

Don't let past failures keep you from future faithfulness. Follow Christ and serve His people going forward. Perseverance in service will ultimately vindicate your usefulness in the cause of the gospel.

# 26

## Honoring Gospel Partners

### Romans 16:3-16

3    Greet Prisca and Aquila, my fellow workers in Christ Jesus,

4    who for my life risked their own necks, to whom not only do I give thanks, but also all the churches of the Gentiles;

5    also *greet* the church that is in their house. Greet Epaenetus, my beloved, who is the first convert to Christ from Asia.

6    Greet Mary, who has worked hard for you.

7    Greet Andronicus and Junias, my kinsmen and my fellow prisoners, who are outstanding among the apostles, who also were in Christ before me.

8    Greet Ampliatus, my beloved in the Lord.

9    Greet Urbanus, our fellow worker in Christ, and Stachys my beloved.

10    Greet Apelles, the approved in Christ. Greet those who are of the *household* of Aristobulus.

11    Greet Herodion, my kinsman. Greet those of the *household* of Narcissus, who are in the Lord.

12    Greet Tryphaena and Tryphosa, workers in the Lord. Greet Persis the beloved, who has worked hard in the Lord.

13    Greet Rufus, a choice man in the Lord, also his mother and mine.

14    Greet Asyncritus, Phlegon, Hermes, Patrobas, Hermas and the brethren with them.

15    Greet Philologus and Julia, Nereus and his sister, and Olympas, and all the saints who are with them.

16    Greet one another with a holy kiss. All the churches of Christ greet you.

Many of us tend to skip the final greetings of the New Testament epistles or to skim them quickly. But taking note of the names and the meaning of the terms can be spiritually profitable.

The term "greet" dominates the last chapter of Romans (16 times in vv. 3-16 alone). It is a command that literally means, "embrace". It carries the idea of "communicate my esteem for" each person mentioned. It is a command to warmly and sincerely honor those named.

In Romans 16:3-5, Paul honors Prisca and Aquila for their labors, their sacrifice, and their commitment to Christ, and the church.

16:5-7—Of Epaenetus Paul writes in effect, "I love him; in Asia it all started with him. Embrace him for me!" "Embrace Mary— remember her hard work." "Embrace Andronicus and Junias, my Jewish kinsmen, those who have been in prison with me, who are well-known among the Apostles, and who were believers even before I was."

16:8—Ampliatus is a Latin name meaning "enlarged". He may have been a man of stature. "Give my love to Ampliatus, who is dear to me in the Lord" (BBE).

16:9—Urbanus was a fellow-worker with the Roman church and Paul. Stachys was another who was specially recognized as close to Paul—his "beloved".

16:10a—The word "approved" speaks of one that has been tested and found to be genuine. "Embrace Apelles, one who has been tested and approved in Christ".

16:10b—Notably, Paul does not greet "Aristobulus" personally, but "those who are *of* Aristobulus". There were some among the "household [perhaps slaves] of Aristobulus" known to Paul. He communicated his affection and encouragement to them.

Space won't permit a fuller exposition of these verses and the rest of the paragraph, but the implications are clear …

In verses 3-15 the Apostle called the Roman church to express his affection for the various individuals and house fellowships mentioned. In 16:16, he called them corporately to express their affection in Christ—for "one another." "*Embrace one another with a holy kiss*" (see also 1 Thes. 5:26; 1 Pet. 5:14—"kiss of love"). Christian affection should be expressed in a culturally appropriate, but *tangible* way.

If you are a believer, you are a partner in the ministry with brothers and sisters in Christ from every economic, social, and ethnic culture in the world. Do we have "dear friends" in the ministry, or just people we sit beside in an audience for an hour a week on Sundays?

This very personal list of instructions and names from two millennia ago reveals the primacy of living our lives to further the gospel of Jesus Christ. Are we fostering relationships with other believers? Are we communicating honor and encouragement to our gospel partners, in our own church and around the world?

May we have a renewed passion for God's work, and a greater affection for God's people.

# 27

## Cuts Like a Knife

### Hebrews 4:11-13

11   Therefore let us be diligent to enter that rest, so that no one will fall, through *following* the same example of disobedience.

12   For the word of God is living and active and sharper than any two-edged sword, and piercing as far as the division of soul and spirit, of both joints and marrow, and able to judge the thoughts and intentions of the heart.

13   And there is no creature hidden from His sight, but all things are open and laid bare to the eyes of Him with whom we have to do.

How many times have we quoted or heard Hebrews 4:12: "For the Word of God is living and active and sharper than any two-edged sword ..." without really knowing the context of the quote and its purpose in the book of Hebrews? The words are so eloquently stated, but without understanding the original intent, its power is misunderstood and misapplied.

The author of Hebrews was exhorting professed Hebrew believers not to return to Old Covenant worship, but rather press on in their New Covenant worship through Christ. Here in chapter four, he called his readers to "be diligent to enter that rest" found in the New Covenant—i.e., genuine trust in God's Word (cf. Heb. 4:3a, 11). If a person fails to enter into God's rest—because he fails to genuinely trust God's Word—then he will fall (as many did in Moses' day).[16]

---

[16] Regardless of which side of the debate you are on concerning whether this passage speaks to the temporal loss of life for a believer or the failure of a professing believer who does not possess genuine faith—this is a clear warning of grave danger.

It is in the context of this grave warning that our beloved text is written. Those who claim to worship God need to make sure they do not disregard God's Word. Why? To disregard God's Word is not simply to reject theoretical ideas and philosophical propositions. Rather, God's Word is alive! It is inextricably bound to the One who is life Himself! To disregard God's Word is to disregard God Himself.

As well, God's Word is active—*energes*. It truly accomplishes the purpose for which God intended it. God said, "Let there be light, and there was light." If God says that those who disregard His Word will fall—then the consequences for unbelief are sure.

The rest of Hebrews 4:12 speaks of the Word of God as a "sword"—a short, dagger-like sword that cuts like a scalpel which is sharper than any known to man. It penetrates the deepest recesses of our being, and it divides what man would consider indivisible.

Therefore, we must not delay in trusting and obeying Christ, Who is the final Word of God to us (1:1-4). Those who refuse to fully follow the Son of God in faith will be judged by Him— because He is the Living Word of God. "And there is no creature hidden from His sight, but all things are open and laid bare to the eyes of Him with whom we have to do" (Heb. 4:13).

For a believer, the Word of God and the promise of God's scrutiny are ultimately a comfort. For we know that He knows we take refuge in Christ for our salvation. Hebrews four ends with the comfort of Christ as our sympathetic High Priest. We can "draw near with confidence to the throne of grace, so that we may receive mercy and find grace to help in time of need" (Heb. 4:14-16).

# 28

## The Other Uriah

### Jeremiah 26:20-23

20   Indeed, there was also a man who prophesied in the name of the LORD, Uriah the son of Shemaiah from Kiriath-jearim; and he prophesied against this city and against this land words similar to all those of Jeremiah.

21   When King Jehoiakim and all his mighty men and all the officials heard his words, then the king sought to put him to death; but Uriah heard *it,* and he was afraid and fled and went to Egypt.

22   Then King Jehoiakim sent men to Egypt: Elnathan the son of Achbor and *certain* men with him *went* into Egypt.

23   And they brought Uriah from Egypt and led him to King Jehoiakim, who slew him with a sword and cast his dead body into the burial place of the common people.

24   But the hand of Ahikam the son of Shaphan was with Jeremiah, so that he was not given into the hands of the people to put him to death.

When you hear the name "Uriah" who do you think of? Most who are familiar with the Old Testament automatically recall the David-Bathsheba debacle, and "Uriah the Hittite," Bathsheba's husband whose death was arranged by David.

The Bible actually mentions several other Uriahs. Perhaps the most intriguing of these lesser-known Uriahs was a contemporary of Jeremiah the prophet. Jeremiah 26:20-23 reveals that this Uriah (alternately spelled Urijah) prophesied against Jerusalem and Judah in the name of Yahweh, much in the same way that Jeremiah did.

When Uriah encountered royal opposition to his message, he fled to Egypt. Judah's king extradited him from Egypt and had him executed. Some speculate that the LORD allowed him to be killed because he fled to Egypt, rather than stay in the land. Later, Jeremiah would warn the remnant against fleeing to Egypt (Jer. 42), but nothing in this text demands such a negative interpretation concerning the martyred Uriah.

If Uriah's death was not a judgment on his actions, how can we explain the fact that he was executed—but Jeremiah (who preached the same message) was not? Simply stated, God had different plans for the two prophets. In fact, it might just be that Uriah's death contributed to Jeremiah's deliverance.

According to the preceding context in chapter 26, Jeremiah was on the verge of receiving a death sentence for his prophetic message of condemnation against Judah and Jerusalem. Some of the officials, however, intervened and spared him that fate by citing previous prophetic announcements that agreed with his message—Uriah's being one of them.

Because other prophets, including Uriah, had confirmed his message, Jeremiah was spared from death at that time. Uriah's message and subsequent murder was evidence that perhaps Jeremiah should not be put to death. Hence, he was spared, and sacred history has been forever altered because of God's grace as recorded in the book of Jeremiah.

"Ahikam the son of Shaphan", mentioned in 26:24, was one of the attendants of the godly king Josiah a generation earlier, when the king heard the Word of God and sought prophetic wisdom as to what would happen to the kingdom. This same Ahikam who had previously played a significant role in turning the nation back to Yahweh was now used to deliver Jeremiah.

No matter how obscure or unknown we may feel, God has a unique ministry and purpose for each of His children. Some may have long and prosperous ministries—others short and difficult, or long and difficult (i.e., Jeremiah). Nevertheless, each is contributing to a brilliantly beautiful, divine tapestry that reveals God's glory in redeeming a people for Himself.

May our Savior grant us the grace to be faithful in whatever ministry He has for us, whether in prosperity or pain—to be used by Him to proclaim the excellencies of Christ.

# 29

## He Who Eats My Flesh and Drinks My Blood

### John 6:53-58

53    So Jesus said to them, "Truly, truly, I say to you, unless you eat the flesh of the Son of Man and drink His blood, you have no life in yourselves.

54    "He who eats My flesh and drinks My blood has eternal life, and I will raise him up on the last day.

55    "For My flesh is true food, and My blood is true drink.

56    "He who eats My flesh and drinks My blood abides in Me, and I in him.

57    "As the living Father sent Me, and I live because of the Father, so he who eats Me, he also will live because of Me.

58    "This is the bread which came down out of heaven; not as the fathers ate and died; he who eats this bread will live forever."

Many, if not most of us, read or hear Jesus' words from John 6 concerning eating His flesh and drinking His blood, and immediately think of communion (a.k.a. the Lord's Supper or the Eucharist). But is this what the passage was intended to primarily communicate?

The previous day, Jesus had fed a crowd of 5000 men with two fish and five barley loaves (cf. John 6:1-13). They were intending, therefore, to make Jesus their king (6:14-15; cf. Deut. 18:15, 18). But as we will see, the rest of John six confirms that they wanted Him as king on *their* terms—not His.

The next day, the crowd found Jesus and asked about His arrival on the other side of the lake. Rather than answer their question, Jesus confronted their motives in seeking Him (6:26-27). They wanted their physical needs met, but Jesus wanted them to understand that their real need was to believe in Him

(6:29). The crowd then began to challenge Jesus to prove that He was able to provide manna for them like Moses had (6:30-31).

Jesus then made His famous pronouncement:

> Truly, truly, I say to you, it is not Moses who has given you the bread out of heaven, but it is My Father who gives you the true bread out of heaven. For the bread of God is that which comes down out of heaven, and gives life to the world … I am the bread of life; he comes to Me will not hunger, and he who believes in Me will never thirst (John 6:32-33, 35).

At this, the people began to grumble, being fixated on their physical expectations rather than the spiritual realities of Christ and His Word. Because of their growing skepticism and unbelief, Jesus challenged even their ability to believe apart from divine enablement (6:36-51).

Finally, Jesus used the shocking metaphor of eating His flesh and drinking His blood to communicate the need to abandon their personal perspective on the physical nature of Messiah's provision—and to utterly rely on Him as the real source of eternal life (6:52-58).

In fact, Jesus had already given a clue as to what it means to eat His flesh and drink His blood. Note the wording of 6:40: "… everyone who beholds the Son and believes in Him will have eternal life, and *I Myself will raise him up on the last day*." And 6:54: "He who eats My flesh and drinks My blood has eternal life, and *I will raise him up on the last day*."

Eating and drinking Christ is a metaphor for seeing Him for who He is, and trusting in Him alone for all of one's needs—physical and spiritual.

There is no direct reference to communion in this passage at all. It took place over a year before Jesus' crucifixion (6:4). The crowd in Jesus' day would have had no understanding of the Lord's Supper whatsoever. No doubt, the recipients of John's

Gospel account would have seen the imagery of the Lord's words and been reminded of the ordinance, but they too would have been forced to grapple with the context and setting. And the context makes it clear that this is not a passage about the ordinance/sacrament. It's about radical trust in Christ as the Bread of Life.

# 30

## Behold, the Kingdom of God Is in Your Midst

### Luke 17:20-37

20  Now having been questioned by the Pharisees as to when the kingdom of God was coming, He answered them and said, "The kingdom of God is not coming with signs to be observed;

21  nor will they say, 'Look, here *it is!*' or, 'There *it is!*' For behold, the kingdom of God is in your midst."

22  And He said to the disciples, "The days will come when you will long to see one of the days of the Son of Man, and you will not see it.

23  "They will say to you, 'Look there! Look here!' Do not go away, and do not run after *them.*

24  "For just like the lightning, when it flashes out of one part of the sky, shines to the other part of the sky, so will the Son of Man be in His day.

25  "But first He must suffer many things and be rejected by this generation.

26  "And just as it happened in the days of Noah, so it will be also in the days of the Son of Man:

27  they were eating, they were drinking, they were marrying, they were being given in marriage, until the day that Noah entered the ark, and the flood came and destroyed them all.

28  "It was the same as happened in the days of Lot: they were eating, they were drinking, they were buying, they were selling, they were planting, they were building;

29  but on the day that Lot went out from Sodom it rained fire and brimstone from heaven and destroyed them all.

30  "It will be just the same on the day that the Son of Man is revealed.

31  "On that day, the one who is on the housetop and whose goods are in the house must not go down to take them out; and likewise the one who is in the field must not turn back.

32  "Remember Lot's wife.

33  "Whoever seeks to keep his life will lose it, and whoever loses *his life* will preserve it.

34     "I tell you, on that night there will be two in one bed; one will be taken and the other will be left.

35     "There will be two women grinding at the same place; one will be taken and the other will be left.

36     Two men will be in the field; one will be taken and the other will be left."

37     And answering they said to Him, "Where, Lord?" And He said to them, "Where the body *is,* there also the vultures will be gathered."

Some English translations of the Bible render Luke 17:21b as "… the kingdom of God is *within* you." This has led many to believe that Jesus was speaking strictly of a spiritual kingdom that exists *inside* one's heart. But the following context in Luke 17 may lead to a different conclusion.

Notice that Jesus was answering the Pharisees' question concerning "when the kingdom of God was coming" (17:20). Certainly as a whole, these men were suspicious of Jesus rather than submissive to Him. Thus, it is clear that Jesus was *not* telling them that the kingdom of God was "within" their hearts.

Next we see Jesus begin to answer their question as to when the messianic kingdom would come. First He told them *how* it would and wouldn't come. It would not come with "signs to be observed" (17:20b). There would be no miraculous sign to herald the actual arrival of the kingdom, but rather it would come suddenly—"Behold, the kingdom of God is in your midst."

Jesus' initial answer may seem a bit ambiguous, in that it could be understood in different ways. But in 17:22-37 He clarified His answer to His disciples. Verses 22-23 indicate that the kingdom would not come immediately as they might have expected. They were not to be deceived by those who say, "Look there! Look here!"

The Kingdom would not come in some localized manifestation that must be discovered. Jesus illustrated what He meant when He said, "Behold, the kingdom of heaven is among you." "For just like the lightning, when it flashes out of one part of the sky, shines to the other part of the sky, so will the Son of Man be in His day" (17:24).

The kingdom of God will not come subtly or gradually. It will come in an instant—and everyone will know it. Just as lightening lights up the sky suddenly and without warning, so will be the coming of Christ to rule the world in glory. Certainly, Christ rules in the hearts of His people. But the question being addressed in this text is the rule of God and His Christ on the earth.

Before that sudden manifestation of God's kingdom however, Christ told his disciples that He must "suffer many things and be rejected by this generation" (17:25). And the world will go on in their willful disregard of the coming kingdom.

As in the days of Noah and Lot, God's judgment will come suddenly and without "signs to be observed" (17:26-33). Only those who believe God and avail themselves of His way of escape will be delivered from judgment and see the kingdom of God come in all its glory. Everyone else will be taken away to judgment (17:34-37).

Are we more concerned about eating and drinking, marrying, buying, selling, and planting than about Christ's return? May God grant us as believers a greater longing for and anticipation of the glorious kingdom of God.

# 31

## Train Up a Child[17]

### Proverbs 22:6

6    Train up a child in the way he should go,
     Even when he is old he will not depart from it.

This beloved verse has been both the hope and the heartbreak of many a parent. Yet the actual meaning of the proverb is debated. Some believe it is a guarantee that no matter how wayward a child may be, if he had been trained to walk with Christ, he will return (even if no one ever knows about it).

Others believe this verse has to do with training a child according to his personality, propensities, and proclivities. This fits nicely in the psychologized world we live in, but is it the intended meaning of the author?

A literal translation of the Hebrew could be rendered, "Initiate a child upon the mouth of his way, even if he grows old he will not change direction." The word "train up" is used of "dedicating" or "inaugurating" the temple, the walls of Jerusalem, etc. It implies setting something in motion that will be its pattern or course in life. The expression, "upon the mouth of" is a Hebrew idiom that speaks of the start or opening of something.

A semi-literal translation would be: "Start a child out according to his way, even if he grows old he will not retreat." Notably, the pronoun, "his" is left to interpretation. But the closest

---

[17] See Dan Phillips's treatment of this verse in *God's Wisdom in Proverbs*, Kress Biblical Resources, 2011.

referent is clearly the "child." There is no explicit mention of God in the text. Could it be that Solomon was using irony to warn against indulging a child's proclivity toward self and sin? "Dedicate from the start a child in *his own* way, and even if he should grow old he will not turn."

Just a few verses later, in Proverbs 22:15 it says: "Foolishness is bound up in the heart of a child; the rod of discipline will remove it far from him." And a survey of the child training verses in Proverbs confirms this idea as well:

- He who withholds his rod hates his son, but he who loves him disciplines him diligently (13:24).
- Discipline your son while there is hope, and do not desire his death (19:18).
- Do not hold back discipline from the child … rescue his soul from Sheol (23:13-14).
- The rod and reproof give wisdom, but a child who gets his own way brings shame to his mother (29:15).
- Correct your son, and he will give you comfort; He will also delight your soul (29:17).

Instead of a promise of a wayward child eventually returning to God, Proverbs 22:6 may be an ironic warning against letting a child have his own way. If a child is consistently allowed to have his own way and thus trained to pursue his own desires from his early youth, it is quite likely that the self-willed child will grow into a self-willed adult.

In the end, believing parents are called to trust God, rely on His grace, model His grace, and thus graciously discipline children from their early youth. And may it be, by God's grace, their children reap the rewards of wisdom and learn to live by faith as well.

# 32

## Barzillai the Gileadite

### 2 Samuel 17:27-29

27  Now when David had come to Mahanaim, Shobi the son of Nahash from Rabbah of the sons of Ammon, Machir the son of Ammiel from Lo-debar, and Barzillai the Gileadite from Rogelim,

28  brought beds, basins, pottery, wheat, barley, flour, parched *grain,* beans, lentils, parched *seeds,*

29  honey, curds, sheep, and cheese of the herd, for David and for the people who *were* with him, to eat; for they said, "The people are hungry and weary and thirsty in the wilderness."

When we think of the great men of faith and faithfulness in the Scriptures, our minds automatically recall the famous men of the Bible like Noah, Abraham, Moses, David, and Elijah, or maybe the Apostle Paul, Peter, or Stephen.

There is a little-known character in 2 Samuel who, because of his generosity and faithful allegiance to God's Kingdom, played a significant role in preserving the Davidic covenant.

David was on the run—not from Saul this time, but from his own son Absalom. David was God's anointed King, but he was suffering from what many would call a self-inflicted wound. He was dealing with the consequences of his own sin with Bathsheba and the murder of Uriah, as well as the consequences of not shepherding his son Absalom as he should have.

Absalom had the support of the nation. Most believed David's time was over. As David left Jerusalem (2 Sam. 15:13ff), he had a band of perhaps 1200 to 2000 supporters, if as it seems likely, women and children went with them (2 Sam. 15:18; cf. 2 Sam. 18:1-4 for an even larger force under David's command by the time the battle came). It was a significant group, but nothing compared to those who supported Absalom, who had won the hearts of nearly the entire nation.

As David went up the Mount of Olives, he left in humiliation and weeping (2 Sam. 15:30). One of his most trusted counselors had defected to Absalom (2 Sam. 15:31). Some were emboldened to even curse him as he left the region, proclaiming that he was getting what he deserved (2 Sam. 16:5ff).

After traveling with this large, but still under-equipped and outnumbered band of refugees, David reached Mahanaim—across the Jordan. As the crow flies it would be at least a 40-mile trek, and it was through hilly terrain. David and his men were tired and on the run.

Second Samuel 17:27-29 records the story of three men, led by Barzillai the Gileadite, who encouraged and financially supported God's King—and thus God's work. The rest of the nation was content with *a* son of David, but not with *the* son of the Davidic covenant. Barzillai, Shobi, and Machir's support allowed David and his men to organize and prepare for the battle that would inevitably come from Absalom.

If you know the story, God providentially worked in Absalom's court to thwart the council of Ahithophel. Providence and the provision of Barzillai gave David the time and resources needed to be ready for the attack.

When Absalom came, David's men won. Absalom was killed. David was restored to the throne. Barzillai sought no reward, no recognition (2 Sam. 19:31-39). His service was for the Lord.

The faith and generosity of supporters played a vital role in redemption history. We worship the Christ—God's Anointed— in part because Barzillai and his two friends took a stand for the truth in supporting David. It could have cost them everything, but they were ultimately loyal to the LORD's King—not the king of the world's choice.

Are we using the resources available to us to support God's mission in this world? As in Barzillai's day, our faith-driven generosity will make a difference.

# 33

## Dogs and Pigs

### 2 Peter 2:20-22

20    For if, after they have escaped the defilements of the world by the knowledge of the Lord and Savior Jesus Christ, they are again entangled in them and are overcome, the last state has become worse for them than the first.

21    For it would be better for them not to have known the way of righteousness, than having known it, to turn away from the holy commandment handed on to them.

22    It has happened to them according to the true proverb, "A DOG RETURNS TO ITS OWN VOMIT," and, "A sow, after washing, *returns* to wallowing in the mire."

Some argue from 2 Peter 2:20-21 that a genuine believer can lose his or her salvation. They focus on the statement that those spoken of "have escaped the defilements of the world by the knowledge of the Lord and Savior Jesus Christ."

The language in and of itself would be fitting for a genuine believer. But then Peter writes in words that speak of judgment: "if ... they are again entangled in them and are overcome, the last state has become worse for them than the first. For it would be better for them not to have known the way of righteousness, than having known it, to turn away from the holy commandment handed on to them" (2 Pet. 2:20b-21).

Chapter two is clearly about false teachers (2:1) and those who follow them (2:2). Admittedly, Peter does indicate that false teachers impact the church, which would include genuine believers (2:3—"in their greed they will exploit *you* ..."). But he makes it crystal clear that God is able to deliver those who are His—from the strongest of believers to the weakest (i.e.,

Noah and Lot; cf. 2:5, 7, 9)—from the judgment that is coming upon the ungodly.

So what did the Apostle mean in 2:20-21 when he speaks of those who have once again been entangled in and are actually overcome by the defilements of the world—*after having* "escaped the defilements of the world by the knowledge of the Lord and Savior Jesus Christ"? The word "knowledge" is *epignosis*—genuine or in-depth knowledge.

The phrase "escaped the defilements" could be translated, "having fled from the pollution." No one can deny that there are at least some who identify with the church, but who are not genuinely regenerate. Can an unbeliever "flee from the pollution of the world" and identify with the church because they have an in-depth, but merely intellectual knowledge of the Lord and Savior Jesus Christ? Again, it would seem clear that the answer is "yes."

In the end, however, it is the last verse of 2 Peter two that clearly identifies these who once fled the world's defilements by the knowledge of Jesus as ultimately unchanged and unsaved. "It has happened to them according to the true proverb, "A DOG RETURNS TO ITS OWN VOMIT," and, "A sow, after washing, *returns* to wallowing in the mire."

These mere professors were not truly sheep, but rather dogs and pigs—unclean animals. For a time they appeared to have changed their ways, but their true character is ultimately revealed by what they return to. Dogs eventually eat their own vomit and pigs eventually live in the mud.

Peter isn't talking about a weak believer like Lot, who often seemed to wallow in the mire and partake of the disgusting ways of the world. He's already made that clear. Rather, Peter is encouraging believers that God will rescue His own, and those who do not belong to Him will ultimately be revealed.

Praise Jesus for His assurance in John 10:27-28: "My sheep hear My voice, and I know them, and they follow Me; and I give eternal life to them, and they will never perish; and no one will snatch them out of My hand."

# 34

## Don't Be Spiritually Paralyzed

### Hebrews 12:12-13

12    Therefore, strengthen the hands that are weak and the knees that are feeble,

13    and make straight paths for your feet, so that *the limb* which is lame may not be put out of joint, but rather be healed.

The book of Hebrews was written for a Jewish audience facing persecution for following Jesus as Messiah, and transitioning to New Covenant worship, rather than remaining under the Mosaic covenant's system of sacrifices and priestly mediation. The great temptation was to go back to the familiar—the Old Covenant's symbols—rather than live in the sometimes-uncomfortable freedom of the New Covenant's reality.

Leading up to chapter 12, the author has made the case that Jesus is superior to everything the Old Covenant could offer. He is greater than the Law and prophets. He is greater than Moses. He has the better priesthood and mediates a better covenant with a better sacrifice. Interspersed throughout the book are warnings to press on in the New Covenant faith of Christ.

Chapter 11 then catalogs the reality that even the Old Testament saints were called to live by faith rather than familiarity. Finally, in chapter twelve, the author speaks of embracing God's discipline rather than running from it.

Then the author wrote the text under consideration: "Therefore, strengthen the hands that are weak and the knees that are feeble, and make straight paths for your feet, so that the limb which is lame may not be put out of joint, but rather be healed." This parabolic statement was meant to communicate the reality that the audience needed to decide to keep following Christ.

The exhortation is to embrace the difficult training/discipline needed to grow in spiritual strength. In their present state of vacillation, they were spiritually paralyzed. The author calls his audience to literally, "straighten up the drooping hands and the paralyzed knees." They were struggling under the threat of persecution and the desire to return to their old way of worship. The answer was to get a grip, exercise their spiritual muscles, and become strong in the faith.

The "straight paths" for their feet is an allusion to Proverbs 4:26: "Mark out a straight path for your feet, stay on the safe path" (NLT). In the context of Hebrews 12, the call is to resume following after Christ, rather than turn aside to the old ways of traditional, Old Covenant Judaism.

If they were not careful to follow the Lord fully, they would not simply be limping around as they were now—their limb would be dislocated. They would be crippled by turning back to the Old Covenant. But in following Christ, their spiritual lethargy and paralysis would be healed.

Many of us today are tempted by the world around us to return to a more socially acceptable form of religion. But the call of the Scriptures is to a radical faith in Christ as God's final Word to us—our Mediator, our perfect sacrifice, and the One who gives us eternal life.

Don't settle for cultural Christianity. Pursue a radical faith in Jesus.

# 35

## Do Not Be Excessively Righteous or Overly Wise

### Proverbs 10:27

27  The fear of the LORD prolongs life,
    But the years of the wicked will be shortened.

### Ecclesiastes 7:15-18

15  I have seen everything during my lifetime of futility; there is a
    righteous man who perishes in his righteousness and there is a
    wicked man who prolongs *his life* in his wickedness.

16  Do not be excessively righteous and do not be overly wise. Why
    should you ruin yourself?

17  Do not be excessively wicked and do not be a fool. Why should you
    die before your time?

18  It is good that you grasp one thing and also not let go of the other;
    for the one who fears God comes forth with both of them.

As Solomon edged toward the end of his illustrious and yet
disappointing reign as King, he wrote a book of wisdom that
serves as an epilogue of sorts to the Proverbs. In the Book of
Proverbs, we see that walking in the fear of the Lord results in
divine blessing. Length of life, material gain, and physical and
spiritual protection, among other benefits, are all connected to
living in the sphere of godly wisdom.

Yet in Ecclesiastes, Solomon communicates the realities of
living in a fallen world. There are apparent contradictions,
anomalies, and other exceptions that don't seem to fit within the
neatly ordered proverbial mindset. So, he wrote Ecclesiastes to
help us process the vanity of life under the sun—life from the
human perspective, apart from God.

There are cases when a man who loves the Lord seems to experience heartache, travail and death, while the wicked man seems to prosper and prolong his life *in his wickedness*. Does this negate the reality that God blesses those who fear Him? No—for there is a judgment to come (Eccl. 12:13-14).

But how do we live in the here and now? How do we fear God without becoming disillusioned with the injustices and contradictions of life under the sun? The aged king had come to understand that we have an amazing propensity to become either self-righteous or sinister in the face of the apparent contradictions to God's goodness and sovereignty.

If we walk in "excessive righteousness," it will ultimately ruin us and those around us. The word "ruin" conveys the idea of being dumbfounded, appalled, or even destroyed. Self-righteousness is destructive to self and others. Those who are overly wise or excessively righteous do not readily embrace the concept of living by faith. There are times when one may seem to be cursed by God, but in reality he is being blessed by God (i.e., Job, Jeremiah, and even Jesus Himself). The self-righteous man can only sit in judgment on such an individual as reaping what he has sown.

On the other hand, some see the apparent contradictions to God's proverbial wisdom and conclude that it really doesn't matter, so why not abandon oneself to wickedness and selfish indulgence. But this approach may lead to an untimely death (Prov. 10:27), even if there are exceptions (as just noted in Eccl. 7:15).

The appropriate response to life in a fallen world is neither self-righteousness nor shameless sin. Ecclesiastes 7:18 counsels dependence on God as you see your own propensity toward both. Solomon is not advocating a little self-righteousness and a little wickedness. He is calling believers to fear God, while hanging on to the knowledge that self-righteousness destroys, and sin leads to death.

When you are feeling the pain of living through injustice or seeing sinners exalted, turn neither to self-righteousness nor to sinister self-indulgence. Trust God even though you can't understand it all. There is coming a day when He will bring about a perfect resolution to all of life's mysteries.

# 36

## God Will Serve Us?

### Luke 12:35-38

| | |
|---|---|
| 35 | "Be dressed in readiness, and *keep* your lamps lit. |
| 36 | "Be like men who are waiting for their master when he returns from the wedding feast, so that they may immediately open *the door* to him when he comes and knocks. |
| 37 | "Blessed are those slaves whom the master will find on the alert when he comes; truly I say to you, that he will gird himself *to serve,* and have them recline *at the table,* and will come up and wait on them. |
| 38 | "Whether he comes in the second watch, or even in the third, and finds *them* so, blessed are those *slaves.*" |

It is clear from passages like Revelation 22:3 that God's people will serve Him for eternity: "There will no longer be any curse; and the throne of God and of the Lamb will be in it, and His bond-servants will serve Him." But have you ever considered the implications of Jesus' parable in Luke 12:35-38?

It must be clearly noted that the main purpose of the parable was to call believers to readiness and faithful service while waiting for Christ's return. But verse 37 paints an astonishing picture of reward for those the Master finds faithful and ready for His return. It says: "Blessed are those slaves whom the master will find on the alert when he comes; truly I say to you, that he will gird himself to serve, and have them recline at the table, and will come up and wait on them."

If this were not Scripture, it would be ridiculous to think that a human master would take on the mantle of a servant and wait on the servants—let alone God the Son Himself waiting on us.

Yet this is what Jesus was stating will be the reward of the faithful.

The phrase, "truly I say to you" in Luke 12:37 emphasizes the statement as true, even if it seems unbelievable. The phrase, "have them recline" combined with "wait on them" contains the imagery of the promised messianic banquet (Luke 13:29; 14:15-24; 22:27:30). At His return, Jesus will actually wait on believers and serve them at the feast. He is the Guest of Honor, who will honor us!

Such glorious grace was present in creation when God created us, made us in His image, and called us to fellowship with Him and to govern His creation (Gen. 1-2). He didn't create us because He needed us. He did so because He is gracious in allowing creatures to experience His glorious character.

God's gracious service was evident in redemption, as God the Son became a man—who came not to be served, but to serve and to give His life a ransom for many (Mark 10:45). And God's grace in serving His redeemed creatures will be evident in glory. As Smedly Yates writes:

> God has always been the servant of His creatures in order to put His own attributes on display. The essence of heaven will be the creature's experience of the excellencies of God. We will revel in who His is. God's attributes do not change from time to eternity. He doesn't stop being gracious, giving, selfless, kind, or overflowing in love when eternity starts. He doesn't stop being an endless fountain that pours out goodness upon goodness upon goodness to people who don't deserve to have any taste of it. And the self-giving nature of God will overflow into countless eons multiplied by infinite ages. This is who our God is.
>
> … Wait on the Lord, and He will wait on you.[18]

---

[18] Yates, Smedly. *Wait: Waiting on God in a World that Won't Wait*, p. 158, The Woodlands, TX: Kress.

# 37

## Andrew

### Mark 3:16-19

16   And He appointed the twelve: Simon (to whom He gave the name Peter),

17   and James, the *son* of Zebedee, and John the brother of James (to them He gave the name Boanerges, which means, "Sons of Thunder");

18   and Andrew, and Philip, and Bartholomew, and Matthew, and Thomas, and James the son of Alphaeus, and Thaddaeus, and Simon the Zealot;

19   and Judas Iscariot, who betrayed Him.

In the parallel accounts of Jesus' choosing of the Twelve Apostles, both Matthew and Luke identify Andrew as Peter's brother and name him just after Peter. But in Mark's record, Andrew is listed fourth (after Peter, James, and John), with no designation as Peter's brother. Yet church tradition strongly suggests that Mark's gospel was written as Peter's account of Jesus Christ's life and ministry.

Perhaps the reason for the omission in Mark 3:18 is as simple as the fact that Mark 1:16 had already identified Andrew as Simon's (Peter's) brother. Whatever the reason, it is encouraging to compile the Scriptural biography of this man who lived in the shadow of his more well-known brother.

According to John 1:37-41, Andrew had been John the Baptist's disciple. He heard and believed John's testimony concerning Jesus as the Lamb of God. Andrew thus began following Jesus. It was Andrew who first introduced his brother Peter to Jesus. In fact John 1:41 says, "He found first his own brother Simon and said to him, 'We have found the Messiah' (which translated means Christ.)" Thus, very early on we see that he was a man of faith, looking for the promised Messiah—and eager to introduce others to Him.

Andrew is always listed among the first four in all the lists of the Apostles in the New Testament, along with the inner triad of Peter, James and John (Matt. 10:2-4; Luke 6:14-16; Acts 1:13; cf. Mark 13:3). But he was not included with them at such events as the raising of Jarius' daughter from the dead (Mark 5:37; Luke 8:51), the transfiguration (Matt. 17:1; Mark 9:1; Luke 9:28), or Jesus' chosen prayer supporters at Gethsemane (Matt. 26:37; Mark 14:33).

The Scriptures further paint an interesting picture of Andrew. As noted, in John 1:41 he first introduced his brother Peter to Jesus. In John 6:8, we find that it was Andrew who brought the boy with five barley loves and two fish to Jesus, just prior to the feeding of the 5000. And in John 12:20-22, it says that it was Andrew who brought some Greeks to meet Jesus, though they had originally approached Philip.

It seems that Andrew was a man who was content not to compete with his brother, or the Sons of Thunder for leadership—but he was a man who consistently introduced people to Jesus. It would seem that Andrew believed that Jesus had the answer to people's needs, problems or questions.

From this brief biblical biography of Andrew, we see that God calls men who quietly serve Him by bringing others to Jesus. He uses people to further His Son's ministry, even if they might appear to be overshadowed by others with more dramatic or dynamic personalities. May we be faithful like Andrew to bring others to Christ, and to serve our Lord with the unique giftedness He has given to us—rather than striving to be someone we are not.

# 38

## The Order of Jesus' Wilderness Temptations

### Matthew 4:1-11

1   Then Jesus was led up by the Spirit into the wilderness to be tempted by the devil.

2   And after He had fasted forty days and forty nights, He then became hungry.

3   And the tempter came and said to Him, "If You are the Son of God, command that these stones become bread."

4   But He answered and said, "It is written, 'MAN SHALL NOT LIVE ON BREAD ALONE, BUT ON EVERY WORD THAT PROCEEDS OUT OF THE MOUTH OF GOD.' "

5   Then the devil took Him into the holy city and had Him stand on the pinnacle of the temple,

6   and said to Him, "If You are the Son of God, throw Yourself down; for it is written,

'HE WILL COMMAND HIS ANGELS CONCERNING YOU';
and

'ON *their* HANDS THEY WILL BEAR YOU UP,
SO THAT YOU WILL NOT STRIKE YOUR FOOT AGAINST A STONE.' "

7   Jesus said to him, "On the other hand, it is written, 'YOU SHALL NOT PUT THE LORD YOUR GOD TO THE TEST.' "

8   Again, the devil took Him to a very high mountain and showed Him all the kingdoms of the world and their glory;

9   and he said to Him, "All these things I will give You, if You fall down and worship me."

10  Then Jesus said to him, "Go, Satan! For it is written, 'YOU SHALL WORSHIP THE LORD YOUR GOD, AND SERVE HIM ONLY.' "

11  Then the devil left Him; and behold, angels came and *began* to minister to Him.

### Luke 4:1-13

1   Jesus, full of the Holy Spirit, returned from the Jordan and was led around by the Spirit in the wilderness

2    for forty days, being tempted by the devil. And He ate nothing during those days, and when they had ended, He became hungry.

3    And the devil said to Him, "If You are the Son of God, tell this stone to become bread."

4    And Jesus answered him, "It is written, 'MAN SHALL NOT LIVE ON BREAD ALONE.' "

5    And he led Him up and showed Him all the kingdoms of the world in a moment of time.

6    And the devil said to Him, "I will give You all this domain and its glory; for it has been handed over to me, and I give it to whomever I wish.

7    "Therefore if You worship before me, it shall all be Yours."

8    Jesus answered him, "It is written, 'YOU SHALL WORSHIP THE LORD YOUR GOD AND SERVE HIM ONLY.' "

9    And he led Him to Jerusalem and had Him stand on the pinnacle of the temple, and said to Him, "If You are the Son of God, throw Yourself down from here;

10    for it is written,

> 'HE WILL COMMAND HIS ANGELS CONCERNING YOU TO GUARD YOU,'

11    and, 'ON *their* HANDS THEY WILL BEAR YOU UP,

> SO THAT YOU WILL NOT STRIKE YOUR FOOT AGAINST A STONE.' "

12    And Jesus answered and said to him, "It is said, 'YOU SHALL NOT PUT THE LORD YOUR GOD TO THE TEST.' "

13    When the devil had finished every temptation, he left Him until an opportune time.

Have you ever heard your father relate an event from his family history, only to hear his brother or sister relate that same event in a slightly different way? All the essential elements were the same, but they were emphasizing different points, and thus their retelling of the episode—though both accurate—differed in some ways. One included details that the other did not. Perhaps one included a detail without reference to the exact chronological order, so as to emphasize why they even brought the story up to begin with.

In like manner—though undergirded and guaranteed by the inspiration of Holy Spirit—the Gospels often relate the same events from different perspectives. Each Gospel has a different purpose for including or excluding certain details.

With that in mind, it is interesting to note the complementary, but different accounts in Matthew and Luke of Jesus' wilderness temptations. The order of the temptations differs.

| Matthew 4:1-11 | Luke 4:1-13 |
|---|---|
| Stones to bread | Stones to bread |
| Jump off Temple | Bow down and worship Satan |
| Bow down and worship Satan | Jump off Temple |

The preceding context in each Gospel account may give us a clue as to why. In Matthew chapter two, Jesus is identified with Israel, as God's Son (Matt. 2:15). Just prior to the temptation account, at the end of Matthew three, Jesus came out of the waters of baptism. This is immediately followed by the statement in 4:1 that he was "led up by the Spirit into the wilderness to be tempted by the devil."

So, Matthew depicts Jesus, God's Son and Israel's representative, as accomplishing what Israel did not. Jesus passed the test in the wilderness after passing through the waters of His baptism. Israel was baptized into Moses, having passed through the Red Sea (1 Cor. 10:2)—but they failed in the wilderness temptation that immediately followed.

On the other hand, Luke places his account of Christ's temptation immediately after a genealogy from Jesus to Adam, the son of God (Luke 3:23-28). This may well be the key to understanding the differences. Adam in Luke's account, like Israel in Matthew's account, is identified as God's "son."

Both Matthew and Luke are contrasting Jesus' faithfulness and victory as God's Son—to those who failed to remain faithful as God's son[s].

The wording of Matthew 4:9-11 seems to identify Matthew's account as holding to the chronological order of the temptations:

[Satan] said to Him, 'All these things I will give You, if you fall down and worship me.' Then Jesus said to him, 'Go, Satan! For it is written, 'You shall worship the Lord your God, and serve Him only.' Then the devil left Him ..."

Why would Luke relate the same events, but not chronologically? Again, it seems he wanted to emphasize the connection and contrast with Adam (Luke 3:23-38). In the Garden of Eden, Adam (God's Son) and his wife failed the test. Genesis 3:6 recounts their fall:

When the woman saw that the tree was **good for food [lust of the flesh]**, and that it was a **delight to the eyes [lust of the eyes]**, and that the tree was **desirable to make one** wise **[boastful pride of life]**, she took from its fruit and ate; and she gave also to her husband with her, and he ate.

Note the parallels in Luke. Satan wanted Jesus to make **food [flesh]; showed** Him all the kingdoms of the earth and promised to give it to Him if He would bow down to him **[eyes]**; and Satan sought to get Jesus to **glorify** Himself **[pride]**.

When tested, God's representative sons, Adam and Israel, failed to love, trust, and honor the Father. But Jesus, the Son of God, honored the Father in every way. Because of this, His redemption and righteousness are effectual to save those who put their trust in Him.

Praise God for the intricate detail of His Word, and for the perfect devotion of His Son (by which we are delivered from our sins)! Gloriously, Galatians declares to believers:

For you are all sons of God through faith in Christ Jesus ... (Gal. 3:26)

But when the fullness of the time came, God sent forth His Son, born of a woman, born under the Law, so that He might redeem those who were under the Law, that we might receive the adoption as sons. Because your are sons, God has sent forth the Spirit of His Son into our hearts, crying, Abba! Father!" Therefore you are no longer a slave, but a son; and if a son, then an heir through God. (Gal. 4:4-7)

# 39

## James—*The* Leader of the Early Church[19]

### Mark 6:3

3    "Is not this the carpenter, the son of Mary, and brother of James and Joses and Judas and Simon? Are not His sisters here with us?"

### John 7:5

5    For not even His brothers were believing in Him.

### 1 Corinthians 15:6-7

6    After that He appeared to more than five hundred brethren at one time, most of whom remain until now, but some have fallen asleep;

7    then He appeared to James, then to all the apostles.

### Acts 1:13-14

13    When they had entered *the city*, they went up to the upper room where they were staying; that is, Peter and John and James and Andrew, Philip and Thomas, Bartholomew and Matthew, James *the son* of Alphaeus, and Simon the Zealot, and Judas *the son* of James.

14    These all with one mind were continually devoting themselves to prayer, along with *the* women, and Mary the mother of Jesus, and with His brothers.

### Acts 12:16-17

16    But Peter continued knocking; and when they had opened *the door*, they saw him and were amazed.

17    But motioning to them with his hand to be silent, he described to them how the Lord had led him out of the prison. And he said, "Report these things to James and the brethren."

---

[19] See William Varner, *The Book of James—A New Perspective*, Kress Biblical Resources, 2011.

## Acts 15:13, 19

13    After they had stopped speaking, James answered, saying, "Brethren, listen to me.

19    "Therefore it is my judgment that we do not trouble those who are turning to God from among the Gentiles ...

## Galatians 1:18-19

18    Then three years later I went up to Jerusalem to become acquainted with Cephas, and stayed with him fifteen days.

19    But I did not see any other of the apostles except James, the Lord's brother.

## Galatians 2:9, 12

9    and recognizing the grace that had been given to me, James and Cephas and John, who were reputed to be pillars, gave to me and Barnabas the right hand of fellowship, so that we *might go* to the Gentiles and they to the circumcised.

12    For prior to the coming of certain men from James, he used to eat with the Gentiles; but when they came, he *began* to withdraw and hold himself aloof, fearing the party of the circumcision.

## Acts 21:18-26

18    And the following day Paul went in with us to James, and all the elders were present.

19    After he had greeted them, he *began* to relate one by one the things which God had done among the Gentiles through his ministry.

20    And when they heard it they *began* glorifying God; and they said to him, "You see, brother, how many thousands there are among the Jews of those who have believed, and they are all zealous for the Law;

21    and they have been told about you, that you are teaching all the Jews who are among the Gentiles to forsake Moses, telling them not to circumcise their children nor to walk according to the customs.

22    "What, then, is *to be done?* They will certainly hear that you have come.

23    "Therefore do this that we tell you. We have four men who are under a vow;

24    take them and purify yourself along with them, and pay their expenses so that they may shave their heads; and all will know that there is nothing to the things which they have been told about you, but that you yourself also walk orderly, keeping the Law.

25    "But concerning the Gentiles who have believed, we wrote, having decided that they should abstain from meat sacrificed to idols and from blood and from what is strangled and from fornication."

26    Then Paul took the men, and the next day, purifying himself along with them, went into the temple giving notice of the completion of the days of purification, until the sacrifice was offered for each one of them.

Based upon a survey of the pertinent New Testament passages, it is commonly acknowledged that James, the Lord's brother, was a recognized leader in the early church. Many have especially noted his leadership within the church at Jerusalem. But a close look at the biblical data seems to indicate that James was likely *the* pre-eminent leader among *all* the church leaders in the early days of the church.

Before Jesus' resurrection, James was a skeptic and scoffer (John 7:1-5). But after seeing the resurrected Lord, James was transformed into a servant of Christ (1 Cor. 15:7; Acts 1:15; James 1:1). Though we can't determine the exact timing of James's rise to leadership, we can see the evidences of it.

After Peter was miraculously released from prison on the eve of his execution, he asked those who were gathered praying for him to tell "James and the brethren" of his release (Acts 12:17). Notice, *James* was mentioned by name.

At the Jerusalem council, after Peter testified of God's grace first coming to the Gentiles through his ministry, *James gave the final word on the matter*, which seems to have been accepted by the leaders at the council: "Therefore it is my judgment that we do not trouble those who are turning to God from among the Gentiles" (Acts 15:19).

Though the Apostle Paul was not a respecter of persons, and certainly would never follow another's lead blindly or without biblical discernment (cf. Gal. 2:9-14), he too seems to have recognized James's leadership. Paul did indeed distribute the letter drafted at the Jerusalem council under James's authority (Acts 16:4).

Moreover, Acts 21:18-26 records Paul's submission to James and the Jerusalem church's leadership in the matter of cultural identification. In order to allay rumors that Paul was calling Jews to abandon mosaic traditions, James and the leadership in Jerusalem called Paul underwrite the expenses for four men under a vow (Acts 21:24). This would be a sizeable expense. Each man fulfilling what would seem to be a temporary Nazarite vow, would have to offer two lambs, one ram, a basket of unleavened cakes and wafers, a grain offering, and a drink offering (Num. 6:13-15). After these were offered, then the men would cut off their hair and burn it on the altar (Num. 6:18). Acts 21:26 says:

> Then Paul took the men, and the next day, purifying himself along with them, went into the temple giving notice of the completion of the days of purification, until the sacrifice was offered for each one of them.

Why is this significant? Beyond the joy of biblical discovery, the evidence concerning James's leadership reminds us of the amazing grace of God. As Jesus' half-brother according to the flesh, James had a privileged life. But those early years were squandered in unbelief. Yet God took a scoffer and skeptic, and transformed him into a servant of the Lord Jesus Christ (James 1:1). There is yet hope for the wayward son or daughter, brother or sister. God's grace is truly glorious!

# 40

## Pursuing the "Deeper" Christian Life

### Colossians 2:6

6    Therefore as you have received Christ Jesus the Lord, *so* walk in Him.

Have you ever felt like your Christian life has become a bit routine—lacking in the joy and vitality it once had? It seems that this tendency is common in believers, as evidenced by many of the encouragements and exhortations in the New Testament epistles. The book of Colossians was written to combat false teaching concerning the ways that a believer's walk with God can be revitalized.

Paul wrote to encourage the Colossian church that knowing Christ was the key to a vibrant walk with God (Col. 2:1-3). There were some, however, who were teaching more supposedly powerful ways of drawing near to Him. Thus, Paul wrote:

> In [Christ] are hidden all the treasures of wisdom and knowledge. I say this so that no one will delude you with persuasive argument ... See to it that no one takes you captive through philosophy and empty deception, according to the tradition of men, according to the elementary principles of the world, rather than according to Christ. For in Him all the fullness of Deity dwells in bodily form, and in Him you have been made complete ... (Col. 2:3-4, 8-10).

Colossians two goes on to detail some of the erroneous ways that were being taught as to how to have greater intimacy with God. These included devotion to religious traditions (2:16-17); the pursuit of mystical experiences (2:18-19); and obedience to man-made rules that have the appearance of godliness but are of no real value in restraining the flesh (2:20-23).

Only finding one's sufficiency and identity in Christ can satisfy the believer's soul. So the key to the Christian life is found in Paul's statement in Colossians 2:6: "… as you received Christ Jesus the Lord, so walk in Him."

How did you "receive" Christ Jesus the Lord? Did you not simply take Him at His Word to save you? Did you not believe that you were inadequate to save yourself—that you could never do anything to make up for past sins and were hopeless in light of your certain sins in the future? But you trusted God's promise to forgive and deliver those who believed in Jesus!

Taking God at His Word is not only the way to enter the Christian life—it is also the way to live it. Continue today, to trust that God's Son is sufficient for you. Christ's death and resurrection mean that *all* of your sins were nailed to cross, and you now have new life in Him (2:10-14).

Those who rest in Christ's Person and work don't need religious traditions or mystical experiences or man-made rules to make them closer to God. Christ has brought us to Himself. And He is God! Take that on faith, just as you did when you first came to the cross—even when you feel less than spiritual. By faith, let the Word of Christ compel you to live for His glory (Col. 3:16-4:6).

You don't need a worldly cocktail of religious traditions, supernatural visions, or rule-keeping asceticism. Keep your eyes on Jesus. He alone saves. And He is at the right hand of God interceding for you.

# 41

## Jesus Learned Obedience

### Hebrews 5:7-9

7   In the days of His flesh, He offered up both prayers and supplications with loud crying and tears to the One able to save Him from death, and He was heard because of His piety.
8   Although He was a Son, He learned obedience from the things which He suffered.
9   And having been made perfect, He became to all those who obey Him the source of eternal salvation.

Though many in Jesus' day struggled to believe that He was indeed *God* incarnate, many of us today struggle with truly believing Jesus was fully *man*. Certainly we agree to it in a doctrinal statement, but we tend to see Him as superhuman—not really subject to the fullness of human impotence and totally beholden to God's hidden providence.

The book of Hebrews, perhaps more than any other book in the New Testament, stresses the absolute necessity of Christ's humanity. If He is not fully man—subject to the creaturely limitations of unfallen humanity—then He is not qualified to be our high priest. If He is not our high priest, we have no representation before God and thus no salvation from God.

But Christ did become a man. He is inscrutably the God-man. He has forever taken on humanity. Thus, He has become our faithful and sympathetic high priest. He represents us before God and has purchased our eternal redemption.

The writer of Hebrews reminds us that Jesus knows what it's like to feel desperate need, to pray, to shed tears of sorrow and pain—and to cry out for help to God (v. 7). Even though He held a unique position as "Son," possessing the very nature, character and attributes of eternal God, "He learned obedience from the things which He suffered" (v. 8). A very literal rendering of the term "obedience" would be, "to listen under."

Jesus *learned* to submit to God's orders. The word "learned" is from the same root as "disciple". As a man, Jesus became an obedient disciple, and suffering played a key role in His discipleship. We see a glimpse of this painful process of learning obedience in Jesus' own testimony recorded in John 12:27: "Now My soul has become troubled; and what shall I say, 'Father, save me from this hour'? But for this purpose I came to this hour. 'Father, glorify Your name.'"

Mark 14:34-36 reveals another glimpse as Jesus told His disciples: "'My soul is deeply grieved to the point of death ...' And he went a little beyond them, and fell to the ground and began to pray that if it were possible, the hour might pass Him by. And he was saying, 'Abba! Father! All things are possible for You; remove this cup from me; yet not what I will, but what You will.'"

Our Lord knows what it is like to live the life of a disciple. He knows the questions, the tears, the pain of living by faith in God, and the path of submission to God's will. And the writer of Hebrews introduced these truths with an application in Hebrews 4:14-16. Since the Son of God also shares our humanity, He can sympathize with our weaknesses. "Therefore let us draw near with confidence to the throne of grace, so that we may receive mercy and find grace to help in time of need."

In your time of need, go to Jesus. He knows. He cares. He will help.

# 42

## Faith

### Luke 7:8-9

8    "For I also am a man placed under authority, with soldiers under me; and I say to this one, 'Go!' and he goes, and to another, 'Come!' and he comes, and to my slave, 'Do this!' and he does it."

9    Now when Jesus heard this, He marveled at him, and turned and said to the crowd that was following Him, "I say to you, not even in Israel have I found such great faith."

### Luke 7:20-23

20    When the men came to Him, they said, "John the Baptist has sent us to You, to ask, 'Are You the Expected One, or do we look for someone else?' "

21    At that very time He cured many *people* of diseases and afflictions and evil spirits; and He gave sight to many *who were* blind.

22    And He answered and said to them, "Go and report to John what you have seen and heard: *the* BLIND RECEIVE SIGHT, *the* lame walk, *the* lepers are cleansed, and *the* deaf hear, *the* dead are raised up, *the* POOR HAVE THE GOSPEL PREACHED TO THEM.

23    "Blessed is he who does not take offense at Me."

### Luke 7:48-50

48    Then He said to her, "Your sins have been forgiven."

49    Those who were reclining *at the table* with Him began to say to themselves, "Who is this *man* who even forgives sins?"

50    And He said to the woman, "Your faith has saved you; go in peace."

### Luke 8:24-25

24    They came to Jesus and woke Him up, saying, "Master, Master, we are perishing!" And He got up and rebuked the wind and the surging waves, and they stopped, and it became calm.

25  And He said to them, "Where is your faith?" They were fearful and amazed, saying to one another, "Who then is this, that He commands even the winds and the water, and they obey Him?"

### Luke 8:47-48

47  When the woman saw that she had not escaped notice, she came trembling and fell down before Him, and declared in the presence of all the people the reason why she had touched Him, and how she had been immediately healed.
48  And He said to her, "Daughter, your faith has made you well; go in peace."

### Luke 8:49-50

49  While He was still speaking, someone came from *the house of* the synagogue official, saying, "Your daughter has died; do not trouble the Teacher anymore."
50  But when Jesus heard *this,* He answered him, "Do not be afraid *any longer; only* believe, and she will be made well."

There is clearly an emphasis on "faith" in chapters seven and eight of Luke's gospel.

- Jesus marveled at the Centurion's faith (7:9).
- John the Baptist sent messengers to Jesus to confirm that He was the Christ—and Jesus pointed to the signs that confirmed His messianic authority based upon Old Testament promises (7:20-23; cf. Is. 26:19; 35:5-6). It was a call to faith in Him as the One who fulfills the Scriptures.
- The forgiven woman was saved by faith (7:48-50).
- The fearful disciples were rebuked for not displaying faith during the storm (8:24-25).
- The woman with the hemorrhage was healed and commended for her faith (8:47-48).
- The synagogue official was called to faith even though his daughter had just died (8:50; "faith" and "believe" are from the same Greek term).

The other events and dialogue in these chapters support and fill in certain details that contribute to this thematic emphasis on "faith" (like "believe", "trust" is a synonymous English term based upon the same Greek word).

- Jesus raised the widow's son from the dead just before He called the disciples of John the Baptist to report to John that the dead are raised (7:11-17).
- Jesus rebuked the Pharisees for their *faithlessness* in rejecting John the Baptist and Jesus as sent from God (7:30-35)
- Jesus' ministry was financially supported by those who had come to *believe* in Him (8:1-3)—much like the woman who had been forgiven.
- The parable of the sower and the soils points to those who hear the word of God with an honest and good heart, and *hold it fast*, and bear fruit with perseverance (i.e., they believe it; 8:4-15).
- The parable of the lamp reveals that those who *believe* God's word will reveal it and be given more light from it. But those who do not have faith—i.e., disbelieve, even what they thought they understood would be taken away from them (8:16-18).
- Those with the *faith* to act on God's Word are considered to be Jesus' closest family (8:19-21).
- The healed demoniac had come to *faith* in Christ as God (Luke 8:39).

If indeed Jesus is the beloved Son, deliverer of mankind (Luke 3:22-38), then the only proper response is to *trust* Him with all that we are and all that we have. In a word, *faith* is the means by which we receive His salvation and see His glory.

We can draw comfort that even those closest to Jesus, who truly believed in Him, struggled with their faith. Indeed, the last chapter of Luke's gospel points again to the central necessity of faith. Jesus rebuked His disciples as He said: "O foolish men and slow of heart to believe in all that the prophets have spoken! Was it not necessary for the Christ to suffer these things and to enter into His glory? … Why are you troubled, and why do doubts arise in your hearts?" (Luke 24:25-26, 38) Whatever trial you may face—even one so dark that there seems to be no way of escape—trust in Jesus and His Word to us in the Scriptures. Faith in His Person, His providence, and His promises is the way of deliverance, forgiveness, and final vindication. Entrust yourself wholly to Jesus.

# 43

## Hezekiah's Response—Haughty or Humble?

### 2 Kings 20:16-19

16 Then Isaiah said to Hezekiah, "Hear the word of the LORD.

17 'Behold, the days are coming when all that is in your house, and all that your fathers have laid up in store to this day will be carried to Babylon; nothing shall be left,' says the LORD.

18 'Some of your sons who shall issue from you, whom you will beget, will be taken away; and they will become officials in the palace of the king of Babylon.' "

19 Then Hezekiah said to Isaiah, "The word of the LORD which you have spoken is good." For he thought, "Is it not so, if there will be peace and truth in my days?"

After Hezekiah's miraculous return to health from a fatal illness, the Babylonian king sent envoys to congratulate him on his recovery and to give him a gift. Second Kings 20:13 records King Hezekiah's response:

> Hezekiah listened to them, and showed them all his treasure house, the silver and the gold and the spices and the precious oil and the house of his armor and all that was found in his treasuries. There was nothing in his house nor in all his dominion that Hezekiah did not show them.

The text goes on to record the prophet Isaiah's rebuke of Hezekiah's actions in 2 Kings 20:16-19.

Hezekiah's response to Isaiah's somber word from the LORD has been much debated: "'The word of the LORD which you have spoken is good.' For he thought, 'Is it not so, if there will be peace and truth in my days?'"

Do the king's words reveal a self-consumed perspective—i.e., "I'm glad that I won't be around for the difficult days of defeat, plunder, and exile in Jerusalem"? Or do they perhaps betray a man who understood God's character and was humbled by His grace?

To support the latter conclusion, we have the inspired statement of Hezekiah's faith and character in summary, found in 2 Kings 18:5-6:

> He trusted in the LORD, the God of Israel; so that after him there was none like him among all the kings of Judah, nor among those who were before him. For he clung to the LORD; he did not depart from following Him, but kept His commandments, which the LORD had commanded Moses.

As well, 2 Chronicles 32:24-26 reveals the divine commentary on this episode:

> In those days Hezekiah became mortally ill; and he prayed to the LORD, and the LORD spoke to him and gave him a sign. But Hezekiah gave no return for the benefit he received, because his heart was proud; therefore wrath came on him and on Judah and Jerusalem. However, Hezekiah humbled the pride of his heart, both he and the inhabitants of Jerusalem, so that the wrath of the LORD did not come on them in the days of Hezekiah.

Hezekiah knew that God was being "good"—i.e., gracious—in postponing exile. He also knew God was righteous in all His ways. When the exile would come in the days of his great grandchildren, God's judgment would be righteous as well.

The chronicler goes on to tell us that God was testing Hezekiah, so that the king might know what was in his heart (2 Chron. 32:31). Even the godliest of men will fail the tests of faith if the Lord is not constantly guiding and protecting their every step. Yahweh let Hezekiah see that. And Hezekiah was appropriately humbled.

Is it any wonder Jesus taught us to pray, "… and lead us not into temptation, but deliver us from evil"? We need the Father's protection every step of the way. Praise Him for His grace and even the tests that reveal our need for His goodness and grace.

# 44

## Paul's Pattern of Teaching the Scriptures[20]

### Acts 9:18-20

18  And immediately there fell from his eyes something like scales, and he regained his sight, and he got up and was baptized;

19  and he took food and was strengthened. Now for several days he was with the disciples who were at Damascus,

20  and immediately he *began* to proclaim Jesus in the synagogues, saying, "He is the Son of God."

### Acts 13:5, 14

5  When they reached Salamis, they began to proclaim the word of God in the synagogues of the Jews …

14  But going on from Perga, they arrived at Pisidian Antioch, and on the Sabbath day they went into the synagogue and sat down.

### Acts 14:1

1  In Iconium they entered the synagogue of the Jews together, and spoke in such a manner that a large number of people believed, both of Jews and of Greeks.

### Acts 16:13

13  And on the Sabbath day we went outside the gate to a riverside, where we were supposing that there would be a place of prayer; and we sat down and began speaking to the women who had assembled.

---

[20] For a fuller treatment of Paul's pattern of evangelism in Acts 17, see Crotts, John. *Upsetting the World*, The Woodlands, TX: Kress.

# Paul's Pattern of Teaching the Scriptures

## Acts 17:1-3, 10-11, 16-17

1      Now when they had traveled through Amphipolis and Apollonia, they came to Thessalonica, where there was a synagogue of the Jews.

2      And according to Paul's custom, he went to them, and for three Sabbaths reasoned with them from the Scriptures,

3      explaining and giving evidence that the Christ had to suffer and rise again from the dead, and *saying,* "This Jesus whom I am proclaiming to you is the Christ."

10      The brethren immediately sent Paul and Silas away by night to Berea, and when they arrived, they went into the synagogue of the Jews.

11      Now these were more noble-minded than those in Thessalonica, for they received the word with great eagerness, examining the Scriptures daily *to see* whether these things were so.

16      Now while Paul was waiting for them at Athens, his spirit was being provoked within him as he was observing the city full of idols.

17      So he was reasoning in the synagogue with the Jews and the God-fearing *Gentiles,* and in the market place every day with those who happened to be present.

## Acts 18:4, 19

4      And he was reasoning in the synagogue every Sabbath and trying to persuade Jews and Greeks.

19      They came to Ephesus, and he left them there. Now he himself entered the synagogue and reasoned with the Jews.

## Acts 19:8-10

8      And he entered the synagogue and continued speaking out boldly for three months, reasoning and persuading them about the kingdom of God.

9      But when some were becoming hardened and disobedient, speaking evil of the Way before the people, he withdrew from them and took away the disciples, reasoning daily in the school of Tyrannus.

10      This took place for two years, so that all who lived in Asia heard the word of the Lord, both Jews and Greeks.

It is clear from the book of Acts that in each of the cities he visited, the Apostle Paul made it his practice to go to a synagogue and teach the Scriptures, proclaiming Jesus as the Christ. An exception is found in Acts 16:13, where it would seem that Philippi did not have an adequate Jewish population to establish a synagogue. Yet even there, Paul went to an alternate place of Jewish worship.

The Jewish synagogue was a place where God's Word was held in high esteem. The gatherings would have been made up of a number of Jews and God-fearing Gentiles, some of whom were likely real believers in the God of the Scriptures, others professed believers, and some perhaps only interested inquirers.

Occasionally a synagogue would allow Paul to continue to teach for months. Others rejected his teaching quickly. Usually there would be some who received the truth of God's Word about Christ with a joyful heart, while others refused to believe. Those who received the Word would be the first fruits of a church in the city. They would continue the work of the ministry after the Apostle's departure.

In Ephesus, after Paul left the synagogue, he went to a "school" where believers and inquirers were allowed to gather as he taught for two years—though the emphasis is clearly on the teaching of disciples, rather than evangelism (Acts 19:9).

On the whole, the Apostle's ministry pattern included teaching the Word of God in places, and to people, who had some knowledge of, and respect for the Scriptures. How might that influence our decisions on how and where to approach ministry and evangelism?

Is there a neighborhood Bible fellowship you could participate in for the purpose of explaining the Scriptures to those who may only have a nominal understanding of them? Is there a business association that is loosely identified as Christian that might be strategic in developing relationships for the gospel's sake? Is there even a church that is open to partnering in some way with your church, that allows opportunities for the Scriptures to be more clearly taught in their midst?

Paul's pattern of ministry was not one that avoided difficulty or opposition. Neither was it a ministry of separation. Like Jesus', it was a ministry that was willing to be criticized and willing to be villainized—if the truth of God's Word, and the glory of Christ were proclaimed.

# 45

## Persistent Prayer or an Honorable Father?

### Luke 11:5-13

5   Then He said to them, "Suppose one of you has a friend, and goes to him at midnight and says to him, 'Friend, lend me three loaves;

6   for a friend of mine has come to me from a journey, and I have nothing to set before him';

7   and from inside he answers and says, 'Do not bother me; the door has already been shut and my children and I are in bed; I cannot get up and give you *anything*.'

8   "I tell you, even though he will not get up and give him *anything* because he is his friend, yet because of his persistence [or "sense of shame"] he will get up and give him as much as he needs.

9   "So I say to you, ask, and it will be given to you; seek, and you will find; knock, and it will be opened to you.

10  "For everyone who asks, receives; and he who seeks, finds; and to him who knocks, it will be opened.

11  "Now suppose one of you fathers is asked by his son for a fish; he will not give him a snake instead of a fish, will he?

12  "Or *if* he is asked for an egg, he will not give him a scorpion, will he?

13  "If you then, being evil, know how to give good gifts to your children, how much more will *your* heavenly Father give the Holy Spirit to those who ask Him?"

While teaching on prayer in Luke 11, our Lord gave two illustrations to highlight His point. Clearly the second illustration focuses on God's goodness and generosity. If it is unthinkable that a father would give his son a snake or a scorpion if the son had asked for a fish or an egg respectively— then it is utterly unimaginable that our heavenly Father would give us anything other than what is supremely good (Luke 11:11-13).

However, the first illustration has been subject to considerable debate. Most translations and interpreters have seen it as a call to persistence in prayer. This is based largely on the application found in verses 9-10: "So I say to you, ask, and it will be given to you; seek, and you will find; knock, and it will be opened to you ..." The imperatives are in the present tense—"keep asking ... keep seeking ... keep knocking".

But why would Jesus put an illustration about persistence immediately next to an illustration about God being much more loving, careful, and thoughtful toward His children's requests than any human father? The illustration about persistence might have negative implications, portraying God as at least somewhat unwilling to answer, needing to be convinced by the persistence of the petitioner.

There is, however, a way to reconcile the two illustrations. The word in verse eight that many English translations render "persistence" is used only here in the Scriptures. It is exclusively used negatively in extra-biblical literature, conveying the idea of "rudeness" or "shamelessness." But clearly, if it refers to the man knocking, it would have to have a positive connotation—i.e., boldness or persistence.

The pronouns in 11:8 could actually convey that the man who initially refused to get up and answer the door would do so—not because his friend was requesting help, but because if he ultimately did not help, *he* (the man being asked) would be seen as shameless and rude.[21]

In other words, even a selfish man has some concern for his honor. How much more then would God be concerned for His honor in answering His friend who is asking, seeking, and knocking?

---

[21] See Johnson, Alan F. "Assurance for Man: The Fallacy of Translating *Anaideia* by "Persistence" in Luke 11:5-8", *JETS*, vol. 22, No. 2 P. 121 June 1979, Logos.

This interpretation then sees both of Jesus' illustrations as supporting the single point that God is concerned about answering His children—because He is truly, intrinsically, and infinitely honorable and good.

We ought to pray with the confidence that God does not have to be cajoled or convinced to answer our petitions. Rather, He is pleased to answer us based upon His own honorable and kind nature. We can boldly ask God to glorify His name in us, help us to submit to His rule, provide for our physical needs, and lavishly forgive us and supply our spiritual needs (cf. Luke 11:2-4).

Keep on asking, seeking, and knocking with that perspective. As we do, we will keep on receiving, finding, and having doors opened for His glory and our good—because He is good, and His honor is at stake.

# 46

## Angels and Demons are Watching

### Job 1:6-8

6   Now there was a day when the sons of God came to present themselves before the LORD, and Satan also came among them.

7   The LORD said to Satan, "From where do you come?" Then Satan answered the LORD and said, "From roaming about on the earth and walking around on it."

8   The LORD said to Satan, "Have you considered My servant Job? For there is no one like him on the earth, a blameless and upright man, fearing God and turning away from evil."

### Job 2:1-3

1   Again there was a day when the sons of God came to present themselves before the LORD, and Satan also came among them to present himself before the LORD.

2   The LORD said to Satan, "Where have you come from?" Then Satan answered the LORD and said, "From roaming about on the earth and walking around on it."

3   The LORD said to Satan, "Have you considered My servant Job? For there is no one like him on the earth, a blameless and upright man fearing God and turning away from evil. And he still holds fast his integrity, although you incited Me against him to ruin him without cause."

### Luke 15:10

10   "In the same way, I tell you, there is joy in the presence of the angels of God over one sinner who repents."

### 1 Corinthians 4:9

9   For, I think, God has exhibited us apostles last of all, as men condemned to death; because we have become a spectacle to the world, both to angels and to men.

### 1 Corinthians 11:10

10   Therefore the woman ought to have *a symbol of* authority on her head, because of the angels.

### Ephesians 3:8-10

8    To me, the very least of all saints, this grace was given, to preach to the Gentiles the unfathomable riches of Christ,

9    and to bring to light what is the administration of the mystery which for ages has been hidden in God who created all things;

10   so that the manifold wisdom of God might now be made known through the church to the rulers and the authorities in the heavenly *places.*

11   *This was* in accordance with the eternal purpose which He carried out in Christ Jesus our Lord

### Ephesians 6:12

12   For our struggle is not against flesh and blood, but against the rulers, against the powers, against the world forces of this darkness, against the spiritual *forces* of wickedness in the heavenly *places.*

### Colossians 2:13-15

13   When you were dead in your transgressions and the uncircumcision of your flesh, He made you alive together with Him, having forgiven us all our transgressions,

14   having canceled out the certificate of debt consisting of decrees against us, which was hostile to us; and He has taken it out of the way, having nailed it to the cross.

15   When He had disarmed the rulers and authorities, He made a public display of them, having triumphed over them through Him.

### 1 Peter 1:10-12

10   As to this salvation, the prophets who prophesied of the grace that *would come* to you made careful searches and inquiries,

11   seeking to know what person or time the Spirit of Christ within them was indicating as He predicted the sufferings of Christ and the glories to follow.

12   It was revealed to them that they were not serving themselves, but you, in these things which now have been announced to you through those who preached the gospel to you by the Holy Spirit sent from heaven—things into which angels long to look.

Excessive speculation about details that go beyond the scope of biblical revelation is neither prudent nor productive (cf. Deut. 29:29), but we *can* contemplate the glimpses of what is otherwise unknown, which *are* revealed in the Scriptures—even if they are not as detailed as we might like.

One such case in point is that angels and demons are revealed as both participants and spectators in the grand drama of God's redemption of sinful humanity. We see this pictured in narrative form in the book of Job. The angels were presenting themselves before the LORD, and Satan was among them, having just come from roaming the earth (Job 1:6-8; 2:1-3). God's challenge to Satan was concerning the irreproachability of His servant, Job. The Slanderer then challenged God, by challenging the motives of His servant—and thus the severe tests began.

There is a spiritual war taking place, not seen with the physical eye. The angels (elect and evil) are watching, and in some ways participating in, a sovereign plan that is unveiling God's glory to these creatures.

The heavenly angels rejoice as they see even one sinner repent (Luke 15:10). Angelic creatures watch the service and submission of God's people—or lack thereof (1 Cor. 4:9; 11:10). And one of the primary functions of the gospel is to reveal God's glory and wisdom in the angelic world, as ethnic and cultural divisions in mankind are overcome by the gospel of the grace in Jesus Christ (Eph. 3:8-10).

As salvation history continues to play out in the human realm, these angelic creatures are seeing aspects of God's glory that they were not privy to simply by being allowed into His presence. Angels stretch their neck, so to speak, to look into how and when God's salvation is accomplished for men (1 Pet. 1:10-12). Ultimately, Christ's resurrection disarmed the demonic authorities and revealed God's triumph over what they likely believed to be their greatest weapons—the debt of sin and its inevitable consequence, death (Col. 2:13-15).

Why does this Spirit-revealed insight into the unseen realm matter to us as believers? We can know that whatever trial, whatever temptation, whatever pain, or whatever opportunity we may face, God's glory is being manifested to this unseen world as we live for Christ by faith.

Even when we are at a complete loss to know why we are struggling with the issues we are struggling with—we can at least know that we are living trophies of God's wisdom and grace on display to the angelic realm.

This insight is not a reason to obsess or to speculate on the unseen spirit world, but it does confirm that our battle is not against flesh and blood, "but against the rulers, against the powers, against the world forces of this darkness, against the spiritual forces of wickedness in the heavenly places" (Eph. 6:12).

Therefore, we must be prepared to stand firm against the enemy with truthfulness, righteous living, and faith, standing firm in the gospel, prayerfully knowing and applying the Scriptures, while we fight this unseen but very real battle (cf. Eph. 6:10-18).

# 47

## The Testimony of Two Servants

### 2 Kings 5:1-3

1 Now Naaman, captain of the army of the king of Aram, was a great man with his master, and highly respected, because by him the LORD had given victory to Aram. The man was also a valiant warrior, but he was a leper.

2 Now the Arameans had gone out in bands and had taken captive a little girl from the land of Israel; and she waited on Naaman's wife.

3 She said to her mistress, "I wish that my master were with the prophet who is in Samaria! Then he would cure him of his leprosy."

### 2 Kings 5:10-14

10 Elisha sent a messenger to him, saying, "Go and wash in the Jordan seven times, and your flesh will be restored to you and *you will* be clean."

11 But Naaman was furious and went away and said, "Behold, I thought, 'He will surely come out to me and stand and call on the name of the LORD his God, and wave his hand over the place and cure the leper.'

12 "Are not Abanah and Pharpar, the rivers of Damascus, better than all the waters of Israel? Could I not wash in them and be clean?" So he turned and went away in a rage.

13 Then his servants came near and spoke to him and said, "My father, had the prophet told you *to do some* great thing, would you not have done *it?* How much more *then,* when he says to you, 'Wash, and be clean'?"

14 So he went down and dipped *himself* seven times in the Jordan, according to the word of the man of God; and his flesh was restored like the flesh of a little child and he was clean.

### 2 Kings 5:15-16, 20-27

15 When he returned to the man of God with all his company, and came and stood before him, he said, "Behold now, I know that there

is no God in all the earth, but in Israel; so please take a present from your servant now."

16 But he said, "As the LORD lives, before whom I stand, I will take nothing." And he urged him to take *it,* but he refused …

20 But Gehazi, the servant of Elisha the man of God, thought, "Behold, my master has spared this Naaman the Aramean, by not receiving from his hands what he brought. As the LORD lives, I will run after him and take something from him."

21 So Gehazi pursued Naaman. When Naaman saw one running after him, he came down from the chariot to meet him and said, "Is all well?"

22 He said, "All is well. My master has sent me, saying, 'Behold, just now two young men of the sons of the prophets have come to me from the hill country of Ephraim. Please give them a talent of silver and two changes of clothes.' "

23 Naaman said, "Be pleased to take two talents." And he urged him, and bound two talents of silver in two bags with two changes of clothes and gave them to two of his servants; and they carried *them* before him.

24 When he came to the hill, he took them from their hand and deposited them in the house, and he sent the men away, and they departed.

25 But he went in and stood before his master. And Elisha said to him, "Where have you been, Gehazi?" And he said, "Your servant went nowhere."

26 Then he said to him, "Did not my heart go *with you,* when the man turned from his chariot to meet you? Is it a time to receive money and to receive clothes and olive groves and vineyards and sheep and oxen and male and female servants?

27 "Therefore, the leprosy of Naaman shall cling to you and to your descendants forever." So he went out from his presence a leper *as white* as snow.

The healing of Naaman, the Syrian general who suffered from leprosy, is beloved among Bible students. In fact, Jesus Himself referenced it when rebuking Jewish unbelief in His day—in His own hometown (Luke 4:27). Naaman is an example of faith outside of Israel, and an example of Yahweh's compassion for Gentiles. But imbedded in the narrative of 2 Kings 5 are the testimonies of faith of several unnamed servants.

The first witness is of a little slave girl who had been taken from Israel in an Aramean raid (5:2). Here was a child who had been kidnapped from her family in Israel. We can only imagine what had happened to her family in the raid. Yet, she believed that there was a prophet in Israel who could help her master Naaman. As she served Naaman's wife, she testified of God's prophet (5:2-3). However simple, there was a genuine element of faith involved in her testimony—and an evident love for her captors.

Next, we see the testimony of more of Naaman's unnamed servants. Naaman had come to Israel in search of the prophet spoken of by his wife's slave-girl. Upon finding him, rather than being greeted with the honor he was accustomed to, Naaman received God's Word from an unnamed messenger of the prophet—which infuriated the great general. Elisha's instructions added insult to injury: "Go and wash in the Jordan seven times ..."

Outraged at being treated like a leper—though he was— Naaman left with every intention of rejecting the word of God's prophet. But 2 Kings 5:13 records that *his servants* came near and spoke to him" and convinced him that he should heed Elisha's word. Their encouragement seems to entertain at least the possibility of faith—if not the proof of it. Naaman listened to their words, obeyed Yahweh's prophet's words, and was miraculously healed by the LORD (5:14).

Having now come to realize that the LORD alone was God (5:15), Naaman returned to honor God's prophet with a lavish gift of silver and gold, and clothing. Knowing that the gifts of God are not purchased, but rather given by grace, Elisha refused to take Naaman's money (5:16). The converted Syrian was no longer angry with Elisha's words, but rather submissive to them.

However, there was yet another servant present, who acts as a foil to the others, however. Gehazi was the *named* servant of Elisha. He was, no doubt, a man well-acquainted with the Word of God. But rather than uphold the honor of the LORD, this servant testified to human greed rather than Yahweh's glory. He secretly followed Naaman and lied to obtain some of the wealth originally offered to Elisha (5:22-24). In doing so, he would bear the reproach of leprosy all of his days (5:27).

The tarnished testimony of selfish ambition and greed will eventually be found out. It renders a man unclean. The testimony of faith may be small and is usually quite simple— but it can change an eternal destiny. God knows the names of the unnamed servants who testify of His glory and grace.

# 48

## Nathan, the Son of David and Bathsheba

### 1 Chronicles 3:5

5　These were born to him in Jerusalem: Shimea, Shobab, Nathan and Solomon, four, by Bath-shua the daughter of Ammiel.

### Matthew 1:1-6

1　The record of the genealogy of Jesus the Messiah, the son of David, the son of Abraham:

2　Abraham was the father of Isaac, Isaac the father of Jacob, and Jacob the father of Judah and his brothers.

3　Judah was the father of Perez and Zerah by Tamar, Perez was the father of Hezron, and Hezron the father of Ram.

4　Ram was the father of Amminadab, Amminadab the father of Nahshon, and Nahshon the father of Salmon.

5　Salmon was the father of Boaz by Rahab, Boaz was the father of Obed by Ruth, and Obed the father of Jesse.

6　Jesse was the father of David the king.
David was the father of Solomon by Bathsheba who had been the wife of Uriah.

### Luke 3:23-31

23　When He began His ministry, Jesus Himself was about thirty years of age, being, as was supposed, the son of Joseph, the son of Eli,

24　the son of Matthat, the son of Levi, the son of Melchi, the son of Jannai, the son of Joseph,

25　the son of Mattathias, the son of Amos, the son of Nahum, the son of Hesli, the son of Naggai,

26　the son of Maath, the son of Mattathias, the son of Semein, the son of Josech, the son of Joda,

27　the son of Joanan, the son of Rhesa, the son of Zerubbabel, the son of Shealtiel, the son of Neri,

28　the son of Melchi, the son of Addi, the son of Cosam, the son of Elmadam, the son of Er,

29     the son of Joshua, the son of Eliezer, the son of Jorim, the son of Matthat, the son of Levi,

30     the son of Simeon, the son of Judah, the son of Joseph, the son of Jonam, the son of Eliakim,

31     the son of Melea, the son of Menna, the son of Mattatha, the son of Nathan, the son of David

Have you ever skipped over the genealogical lists of mostly unpronounceable names in the Bible? You're not alone. But they contain vital information that confirms the prophetic fulfillment of God's Word and the faithfulness of God's promises.

First Chronicles 3:5 records the sons who were born to David in Jerusalem: Shimea, Shobab, Nathan and Solomon, four, by Bath-shua the daughter of Ammiel. "Bath-shua" is a variant spelling of Bathsheba. "Ammiel" is a transposed spelling of the name "Eliam" (cf. 2 Sam. 11:3).

This genealogy tells us that David had four sons by Bathsheba—and two of them are listed in the two New Testament genealogies of Jesus! Matthew's genealogy record's Jesus' legal lineage through David's son Solomon. It confirms Christ's right to rule as the Davidic King. Luke's genealogy traces Jesus' actual human genealogy, through David's son Nathan, and goes all the way back to Adam (Luke 3:23-38).

Though they are *difficult* to reconcile, the two different lists are *not contradictory*. Jeremiah 22:30 prophesied that Jeconiah (a king from David's lineage) would *not* have a son sit on David's throne or rule again in Judah. In Matthew's list, Jeconiah's son is Shealtiel (Matt. 1:12; cf. 1 Chron. 3:17). In Luke 3:27, Shealtiel is named as a son of Neri.

According to Jewish law, a brother who died childless could raise up an heir that would inherit his brother's name and legal right. It may well be that Jeconiah had no heir, but Shealtiel became his heir through a levirate marriage or perhaps adoption. This would insure that the prophecy was fulfilled, yet account for the genealogical record.

Nathan and Solomon were both sons of David by Bathsheba (1 Chron. 3:5). Their family trees separated and then met again in Shealtiel and his son Zerubbabel. They parted again thereafter (Matt. 1:12; Luke 3:27). Notably, it would seem that by the time of the prophet Zechariah, David's son *Nathan* (through his descendants) would play a role of significance in the Davidic family tree (Zech. 12:12).

Matthew highlight's Jesus' legal genealogy and right to rule through Joseph (via Solomon). Some have suggested that Luke is Jesus' genealogy through Mary, whose father was "Eli" (note Luke 3:23—"as was supposed the son of Joseph" [but actually] "the [grand]son of Eli"). Though Mary is never explicitly mentioned as part of the genealogy, the fact that the list goes from Jesus back to Adam seems to confirm that Luke was tracing Christ's human lineage. And Luke had already established that Jesus' humanity was a special creation by the Holy Spirit in Mary's womb (Luke 1:30-35).

Jesus' two genealogies confirm that He is the promised son of David who has the right to rule as King of Israel, and the promised son of man (Adam means man) who came to redeem the sons of Adam. And amazingly, both his legal lineage and human lineage seem to be connected to different sons of David born to *Bathsheba*.

Every word of God is tested. He is a shield to those who take refuge in Him. If we were recording Jesus' lineage, we might be tempted to either skip the detail, better synchronize the names— and perhaps leave out the facts that remind us of David's royal scandal. But the Holy Spirit is not a man and does not think as a man. He has given us enough information to remind us of God's grace to sinners and yet call us to live by faith. Glory in God's penchant for the details as well as in His plan of deliverance through Christ!

# 49

## No Vacancy—Or Not Welcome?

### Luke 2:6-7

6    While they were there, the days were completed for her to give birth.

7    And she gave birth to her firstborn son; and she wrapped Him in cloths, and laid Him in a manger, because there was no room for them in the inn.

Was there really a "no vacancy" sign on the Bethlehem Inn some 2000 years ago when Jesus was born?

Actually, the Greek word for "inn" in Luke 2:7 refers to a "guest room". It is used in Mark 14:14 and Luke 22:11 to refer to the "upper room" or "guest room" in which Jesus and His disciples ate the last supper.

Why was there "no room" for Joseph and his expecting, betrothed wife? It is possible that the census had caused Bethlehem to swell beyond its capacity to hold even two more visitors. But there could be little doubt that Joseph had relatives in Bethlehem, since he was of the family of David. Did no one have even a small space to give the couple?

It is very possible that news of Mary's untimely pregnancy had reached relatives in Bethlehem well before Joseph and Mary did. Could it be that Luke 2:7 is not speaking of an "inn" as in a shelter specifically for travelers, but rather a "guest room" in one of Joseph's relatives' homes?[22]

Though we can't know for sure, we do know from John 8:41 that Jesus' conception and birth were consider scandalous by some, when the crowds "said to Him, 'We were not born of fornication ...'" And later, "The Jews answered and said to Him, 'Do we not say rightly that you are a Samaritan and have a demon?" (see also John 9:29). It would seem that rumors regarding Jesus' birth followed Him.

For whatever reason, when the time came for Mary to give birth, there was no room for a pregnant woman to have her baby. But someone did evidently allow her and her husband to use the room, shelter, cave, or area outside where the animals were kept. It is possible that the animal room was an additional room on the house, next to or perhaps under the family's living area.

And so was the inglorious birth of God's Son. Whether "no vacancy" or "not welcome," Jesus was born in obscurity and without fanfare—except for the angelic announcement to shepherds (who were definitely not high on the social ladder in their world).

God often works in unexpected ways, through seemingly insignificant people, under apparently inglorious circumstances. We need to let the Scriptures inform our understanding of significance and success. Knowing that Jesus was not particularly welcomed by most from birth should help us understand why those who follow Him are not welcome in this world.

---

[22] In the parable of the "Good Samaritan" a different term is used for "inn".

Our Lord was born in a less-than-exalted setting, so that through His perfect life, substitutionary death, and triumphant resurrection we could be born from above and be exalted with Him in heaven.

# 50

## The Good News of a Crushed Skull

### Genesis 3:15

15    And I will put enmity
Between you and the woman,
And between your seed and her seed;
He shall bruise you on the head,
And you shall bruise him on the heel."

Did you know that the first prophecy of Christmas in the Scriptures included the promise of war and a crushed skull? The Bible in Basic English captures the essence of Genesis 3:15 with its paraphrastic translation: "… there will be war between you and the woman and between your seed and *her seed*; *by him* will your head be crushed" (emphasis added).

Normally, descendants are counted as the "seed" or offspring of the father. In this prophecy, however, God promised that there was coming a unique "seed" or "offspring" of the woman who would deal a death blow to the Serpent—the very one who led man into sin and death.

"Seed" is a collective singular, which can refer to "seeds" plural—or "seed" singular. Clearly an individual in view in this prophecy, as the pronoun "him" (singular) is used for the One who would "bruise" or "crush" the head of the Serpent.

Think about the context of this prophecy for a moment. Adam and Eve lived in a perfect world, with a perfect marriage, and a perfect relationship with God. There was no sin, no sin nature, no fallen world to skew reality. Yet they were by no means victorious over temptation, sin and death. They abdicated their created role as the God-appointed rulers of creation to the serpent. Adam and Eve submitted to the serpent's word rather than God's Word.

Certainly that first couple knew of only One Being who could defeat their enemy—God Himself, the LORD (Yahweh). Yet that One Being was promising that there was coming a "seed" of the woman who would defeat Satan. What would Adam and Eve have understood about this prophecy?

Could it be that they knew that somehow, inscrutably, there was coming a child—a man—who would possess the character, nature, and attributes of God Himself? Could it be that they understood Yahweh to be promising the incarnation of God—the God-man?

The first clue comes in Genesis 3:20. After being told that life would be full of toil and pain, and that he would eventually die physically (Gen. 3:17-19), Adam "called his wife's name Eve, because she was the mother of all the living." Though he knew spiritual death personally—separation from Yahweh and his wife—Adam called his wife's name "Eve," which means "life".

Adam evidently believed Yahweh's promise. Yahweh, the Giver of life, was promising that Eve would give birth to One who would restore life to this now-fallen creation.

The birth of Cain recorded in Genesis 4:1 may also give a clue to Eve's faith, as the grammar allows and could actually indicate that Eve believed Cain might be the promised God-man. Though this is debated by scholars, it is clear from Isaiah 7:14 as well as other passages that the believing remnant in

Israel was looking for the God-man to come and deliver His people from the power of sin and death.

Christmas is about a war—won by Christ, the God-man. He was wounded for our transgressions. But He crushed the head of the serpent in His victory over death. The New Testament promises that He will soon crush Satan under your feet as well (Rom. 16:20). In other words, believers will experience that same victory in their war with Satan, because of Christ.

# 51

## The *Three* Wise Men?

### Matthew 2:1-12

1     Now after Jesus was born in Bethlehem of Judea in the days of Herod the king, magi from the east arrived in Jerusalem, saying,

2     "Where is He who has been born King of the Jews? For we saw His star in the east and have come to worship Him."

3     When Herod the king heard *this*, he was troubled, and all Jerusalem with him.

4     Gathering together all the chief priests and scribes of the people, he inquired of them where the Messiah was to be born.

5     They said to him, "In Bethlehem of Judea; for this is what has been written by the prophet:

6          'AND YOU, BETHLEHEM, LAND OF JUDAH,
            ARE BY NO MEANS LEAST AMONG THE LEADERS OF JUDAH;
            FOR OUT OF YOU SHALL COME FORTH A RULER
            WHO WILL SHEPHERD MY PEOPLE ISRAEL.' "

7     Then Herod secretly called the magi and determined from them the exact time the star appeared.

8     And he sent them to Bethlehem and said, "Go and search carefully for the Child; and when you have found *Him,* report to me, so that I too may come and worship Him."

9     After hearing the king, they went their way; and the star, which they had seen in the east, went on before them until it came and stood over *the place* where the Child was.

10    When they saw the star, they rejoiced exceedingly with great joy.

11    After coming into the house they saw the Child with Mary His mother; and they fell to the ground and worshiped Him. Then, opening their treasures, they presented to Him gifts of gold, frankincense, and myrrh.

12    And having been warned *by God* in a dream not to return to Herod, the magi left for their own country by another way.

Were there really *three* wise men who came to visit the baby Jesus shortly after His birth? We may be tempted to imagine three lone men riding camels as they followed the star toward Israel. But Matthew 2:1-12 paints a fuller picture.

The idea of "three" wise men comes not from a direct statement in the text, but an inference from the three gifts that were given—"gold, frankincense, and myrrh." But clues in the narrative indicate that there was likely a significant entourage that arrived in Jerusalem looking for the newborn King.

Note that verse 3 says, "When Herod the king heard, he was troubled, and all Jerusalem with him." Jerusalem was a very significant city located at the hub of trade and travel between Egypt and Mesopotamia. They no doubt were used to bands of travelers. A few visitors talking about a star and a king might have been a bit novel to some, but would not likely draw the attention of the region's "king" and "all Jerusalem".

But a band of foreign dignitaries with a small militia for traveling protection would have caused quite a stir. Though "magi" were not "kings," they were likely an elite guild of men known for their academic and religious pursuits, and perhaps their role as political advisors (cf. Dan. 1:20; 2:2, 10, 27; 4:7; 5:7, 22, 25; 5:11). Whatever their exact function in their world, their arrival in Jerusalem got the attention of the highest official in the entire region and caused a stir in the whole city. In fact, their presence and their quest issued in a personal audience with King Herod himself (v. 7).

Beyond these considerations, it is helpful to understand Matthew's purpose in recording their visit in his Gospel account. It is clear that Matthew wrote for a Jewish audience. He began with Jesus' lineage from Abraham (Matt. 1:1) and ended with a clear allusion to the Abrahamic covenant promise of blessing to all the nations (Matt. 28:18-20). Yet Matthew tends to highlight the faith of Gentiles (cf. 1:5, 6; 2:1-2, 11; 3:9; 4:15-15; 8:5-12; 11:17-21; 12:38-42; 15:21-28; 24:14; 27:54; 28:19). In a sense he has written as an apologetic (a reasoned defense) for the inclusion of Gentiles in God's kingdom plan.

The "magi" came to Israel's Messiah as worshippers, while those who should have been looking for Messiah were "troubled." The "chief priests and the scribes" in Israel knew the Scriptures but were not compelled to find the Christ. Herod wanted to find Him and kill Him, because this one was born King of the Jews.

Though limited in their access to the truth of Scripture, these men followed the light given them (literally and figuratively speaking). They were privileged to worship and serve the Messiah. Their gifts of gold, frankincense and myrrh may well have financed Jesus' family's stay in Egypt.

Some hear about Christ and try to eliminate Him in fear of losing their sovereignty. Others know the truth about Christ intellectually, but do not seek Him out. But those who believe, seek to worship and serve Him. Which best describes you?

# 52

## Overcoming the World

### 1 John 5:3-5

1   Whoever believes that Jesus is the Christ is born of God, and whoever loves the Father loves the *child* born of Him.

2   By this we know that we love the children of God, when we love God and observe His commandments.

3   For this is the love of God, that we keep His commandments; and His commandments are not burdensome.

4   For whatever is born of God overcomes the world; and this is the victory that has overcome the world—our faith.

5   Who is the one who overcomes the world, but he who believes that Jesus is the Son of God?

The larger context of 1 John 4-5 emphasizes the inseparability of love (for God and other believers), faith in Christ, and obedience to God's Word. Those who genuinely have fellowship with God through faith in Christ (1:1-4), and thus eternal life (5:11-13), are characterized by these three realities. But what is the love of God?

First John 5:3 tells us that "this is the love of God, that we keep His commandments." Yet this obedience to God's Word is not a works-righteousness pursuit of gaining His love. Rather, this is a love-driven obedience that truly believes in who Jesus is and what He has done.

Note the explicit connection: "for this is the love of God, that we keep His commandments; *and His commandments are not burdensome*" (emphasis added). "Burdensome" speaks of that which is an oppressive load. John is thus repeating what Jesus

164

had explicitly stated—God's commandments are not an oppressive load (Matt. 11:30).

From the very beginning, one of Satan's primary tactics is to delude man into thinking that God's commands are burdensome (Gen. 3:1-5). Ever since that first day of the Fall, the world system has believed this demonic lie. But we have the great promise that "whoever trusts that Jesus is the Christ is born of God ... [and] whatever is born of God overcomes the world" (5:1, 3).

The word "overcomes" is from the Greek term that gives us the word Nike. It means "to have victory over" or "to conquer." Those who trust in Jesus Christ have victory over the world's deluded thinking. We trust that God's Son has come to rescue from our sin. He shed His own life's blood to deliver us from the wrath that we deserved (2:1-2).

God's commandments are a burden to those who are blinded by worldly thinking.

> "Worldly thinking tells us that it is not in our best interest and for our ultimate good that we obey God's Word. But the truth is that God wants only the very best for us. When a person comes to Christ ... through faith, God gives him or her the power to gain victory over the world and its mindset. Faith (submissive trust in Christ) conquers worldly thinking."[23]

The one who truly believes that Jesus is God come in the flesh, and that He has come to pay for our sins and has risen from the grave—this one overcomes the world and its thinking. Such faith issues in love. And love lightens the burden (Gen. 29:20) as we live for the One who has loved us so.

Overcoming the world does not mean that we are somehow exempt from life's problems. Rather, it means that we have overcome the world's perspective on those problems. We are

---

[23] Kress, Eric, *Notes for the Study and Exposition of 1st John*. The Woodlands: Kress, p. 112.

ultimately victorious over our fleshly rebellion and disobedience to God's Word.

If you feel that obeying God has become a burden, go back and prayerfully remember Who Jesus is and what He has done—*for you*. Ask God's Spirit to strengthen you with a faith-driven resolve to love God in obedience to His Word, and to love others as you have been loved.